# A WEALTH OF FAITHS

Published by World Wide Fund for Nature UK (WWF) Education Department.

© 1992. NEF, WWF UK, and Christian Aid.

ISBN 0-947613-85-4

Photographs
All colour photographs are reproduced with the permission of Circa Photo-library, c/o ICOREC.
Colour photography; John Smith, Martin Palmer, Barrie Searle, Mike Edwards, Ged Murray, Ranchor Prime.
Black and white photographs: Ged Murray; pages 6, 7, 8, 14, 15, 17, 25, 32, 57, 58
Profile Photo Agency, John Smith; pages 32, 40, 57, 58.
Barrie Searle; pages 50, 51.

Designed by Caro Inglis
Illustrations by Brent Linley
Typeset by Point to Point, New Mills.
Printed by Shanleys, Bolton.
Printed on chlorine-free, environmentally friendly paper.

# CONTENTS

# Acknowledgements

The authors of the book wish to express their gratitude to the many members of the religions represented in this book, who gave us so much time and effort. Over a period of two years, religious leaders, economic specialists, educators and scholars gave their time and knowledge to further this work. There are too many to name, but our heartfelt thanks to all who helped.

Our appreciation to our colleagues within the New Economics Foundation, especially James Robertson, Pat Saunders and John Davis who have worked with us throughout the period of this project. A special thanks also to Ed Mayo.

From Christian Aid, Barbara Vellacott's support and insights have been greatly appreciated. In WWF, the enthusiasm and help of Ivan Hattingh has helped make the project possible.

Finally, our thanks go to our colleagues in ICOREC, especially Jo Edwards and Liz Breuilly and in particular to the resources of the Circa Photo-library, part of ICOREC, which provided the photographs.

# How much are you worth?

Rabbi Soloman had never owned a house or saved any money. One of his greatest pleasures was to travel and whenever he heard stories of foreign towns he packed a small bag containing books and some clothes and set off on his journeys again.

On one sea journey Rabbi Soloman ended up travelling with a group of wealthy merchants. The journey took two weeks and by the end of the first week the passengers were tired of the hot sun and bored by the sight of endless ocean. Each evening the passengers discussed and argued whatever issues came into their heads. One night the merchants were boasting about what they owned and how much their goods were worth. Rabbi Soloman said nothing to the merchants and eventually they turned to him, thinking he was a merchant.

"What goods do you have to sell and how

much are you worth?" they enquired.

"My goods are more valuable than all the rest of your goods put together," replied Rabbi Soloman mysteriously.

The merchants were astonished at this and demanded:

"What are your goods? Why are they more valuable than ours?"

But the rabbi said nothing. Soon the merchants began to mock the rabbi.

"You're lying to us. You don't have anything of real value. In fact you probably own nothing more than the clothes you stand up in."

Three days later, when they were still far out in the ocean, the ship was attacked by pirates. They swiftly overwhelmed the sailors and stole everything on the ship. All the goods, all the personal treasures, even the clothes the people were wearing. It was two days later when the ship limped into a foreign port. The merchants knew no-one in the city and had no money to eat or pay for a room. The rabbi, however, went straight to the local synagogue and study house.

There he was welcomed as a member of the faith. Once he began to teach, he was showered with gifts, good food and offers of hospitality. The next day, the merchants were wandering sadly along the street when the rabbi passed them, well dressed and surrounded by new friends.

"Now we see that your goods are of greater value than our gold, fine jewels and cloth," they said. "We begin to realise that learning is the best form of goods."

Ever since time began, some people have judged others more by what they had than by what they were. Is this the only way that we value other people? You probably value your friends, your parents, the adults who care for you, perhaps a good teacher or a religious leader. Maybe you value a footballer, tennis star or some other person who does well in a sport you like. When we say we 'value' someone, it usually means we like them for what and who they are. It doesn't usually mean we value them in terms of just money.

# ACTIVITIES

1. Here is a list of jobs that could be found in the area where you live. Think of three more jobs that you can add to this list.

   | | |
   |---|---|
   | Bank Manager | Farmer |
   | School cleaner | Vet |
   | Solicitor | Social Worker |
   | Sports Teacher | Shop assistant |
   | Binmen | Nurse |
   | Estate Agent | Gardener |
   | Doctor | |

   a. Number these jobs in what you think should be the order of importance. The one you feel is most important should be number one and the least should be number 14.

   b. List who you think should be the best paid and who should be the least. Why have you put the jobs in this order? What things about each job did you feel were most important? What did you value most in the different jobs?

2. Look at the adverts in colour supplements or magazines. Sort out the adverts into two groups.

   a. Those that are trying to help you or give information.

   b. Those that are just trying to sell you something.

♦ *Policemen on duty at a demonstration.*

Imagine you are a traveller from space and these adverts are all you have to help you understand the world. What would you think about the world from your first set of adverts? What would you think from your second set of adverts? How do the 'worlds' differ from each other?

What we do with money, what we think is important to spend money on, and how we treat others are all called 'values'. They tell us a lot about what is most important to us and to our society, even at times to our world. For instance, some governments of the world spend more money on weapons and armies than they spend on health, education and housing combined. It doesn't take too much imagination to see what the rulers of those countries think is important. Think about your own local town or city. Probably over the last few decades there has been a lot of rebuilding in the centre. New shopping centres for instance. Perhaps at the weekend you could go and look at your town or city centre. Imagine being an elderly person, or a mother or father with a baby in a push chair and a toddler on reins. How easy would it be for you to get around the new bits of town, the new shopping centre or other areas? You can soon see who the new bits of a town have been built for. In our city, people have said that our new shopping centre is designed for young men and women in their twenties who are healthy, have lots of money and no children.

If you look beyond your home town or country it is possible to see how the natural resources are being used or abused by those with power. Listen or watch the news for a couple of days and mark down all the items on the environment that you hear. Items like floods caused by chopping down trees; worry about the 'greenhouse' effect or the ozone layer; deaths of animals and so on. Then think about all the resources you use in your house, in your school, in your area, which cannot be used again – non-renewable resources as they are known. Things like oil, petrol, coal, certain types of woods, stones, land and so forth. If you think about it, we are using up the world. The big question is, how much longer can we do this. The way we live today means there may not be a world for us to live in tomorrow. We cannot go on using resources as if they will never run out. They already are! We cannot go on trying to get more and more wealth when this is literally costing us the earth. In order to stop this we may have to change the way we live and to think again about the things that are important in our life.

We need to start looking not just at what we are doing but at why we do things. This brings us to the area of what we believe. Many of you will not have specific beliefs, while some of you will be Christians, Muslims, Jews, Hindus and so on. Whatever you do or don't call yourself, you have beliefs. You believe certain things are right, certain things wrong. Perhaps even more important, you accept a lot of things around you as simply being 'how things are'. But who says that things should be as they are? Why do we continue to live in a way that threatens the world we all love? Why do we use materials which cannot be replaced, which pollute the world or which are only produced at great cost to other people around the world?

In the following pages you will meet a number of people who, in very different ways, are trying to answer these questions. All of them hold strong beliefs and from these beliefs they try to make sense of the world. You also have your beliefs. We hope that as you read the stories and explore the beliefs which lie behind them, you can think a bit about what you believe and do. You may find some ideas, some ways of behaving or thinking that you read about in this book interest you. You may feel that some ideas could be helpful to you. Or you may just feel pleased that so many people, for so many different reasons, care – just like you.

# BUDDHIST STORY

David ran to Anna's side and she could tell something was wrong. "They've gone towards the hut. I couldn't stop them. They thought it would be a good place to hide," he said as he cast glances back to where the three other children had gone.

"Well I told you it was a stupid idea to play in this part of the woods. Now we will have to stop them," replied Anna, looking very angry.

"Do you think they will find him?" asked David.

"I hope not," said Anna as she began to run into the woods and towards the hut.

As David ran after her he could have kicked himself for being so silly. It was his idea to play hide and seek in the West Woods. Normally they played down by the stream in Middle Wood. But West Wood was more densely planted with trees. And he had forgotten entirely about the hut and the monk.

The other three were almost upon the hut when Anna called out to them. The anxiety in her voice held them back and they came back through the woods to the small hill where she stood.

"There's a what?!" said Andy after Anna had explained why they couldn't go near the little hut.

"There's a Buddhist monk in the hut and he mustn't be disturbed," said David.

"Well what's he doing there?" asked Joanne.

"He's meditating and he will stay there for about three months. We bring him his food once a day. Other than that, no one comes near him," replied Anna.

Joanne was not impressed. "But where's he come from?" she demanded. "This is England, Surrey. England, not . . . not China or Thailand."

Anna replied, "Surely you know about the Buddhist monastery at Chithurst. They've been there years. They follow Thailand's kind of Buddhism – but many of them are English or American. Well, he comes from there."

"Is he some sort of beggar?" asked Steve.

"No. It's not like that," answered Anna. "As you know, our mum and dad are Buddhists. They believe that the monks have something very special to share with us and keep for us. Something much more valuable than gold. The monks keep the teachings of the Buddha alive for us and teach us how to live. In return we offer them food. This means they don't have to worry about money or buying things. They lead a simple life and we give them what they need. So, they can concentrate on the teachings of the Buddha."

"What! You mean they don't have any money – not even pocket money?" asked Steve.

"Not a penny. Mum says they have the great treasure of the Buddha's teachings," said Anna.

"Sort of 'Guardians of the Great Treasure'" said Joanne, who liked role play games and often invented phrases like that.

"I suppose it is a bit like that," said David. "Dad says the Buddha is like a Jewel. He talks about the Three Jewels. It goes like this:

'I take refuge in the Buddha;

I take refuge in the Dharma;

I take refuge in the Sangha.'"

"Sounds a bit funny to me," said Andy. "What does it mean?"

"Well, as I understand it, Buddhists believe that the Buddha found the secret of why people suffer. He said we suffer because we always want to hold onto things," said Anna. "Like today. Today is a beautiful sunny day in the holidays. We are enjoying it and yet part of us is wondering when it will end and is feeling sad that it will end. Life is like that. Everything passes away; everything dies or decays. Nothing remains the same. But we keep trying to pretend that things can stay the same. When they don't, we feel sad and we suffer."

"But what's that got to do with your monk in his hut?" asked Joanne.

"It goes back to that Three Jewels business. The monks are part of the three Jewels," said Anna. "The teaching of the Buddha is called the Dharma – the second of the Three Jewels. The Buddha taught that there are four steps on the way to escaping suffering, called the Four Noble Truths. In these four truths he also taught eight steps on the path to living according to his teachings. I'll lend you a book on the Four Noble Truths and the Eightfold Path. Basically the eightfold path shows us how to live; what jobs are good; what behaviour is good and so on."

"So that's the Buddha and the teachings – the Dharma. But what about the monks?" asked Steve.

"I'm coming to them," said Anna. "The monks keep the knowledge about the Buddha and his Dharma alive. They live as simply as possible in order to concentrate on the Dharma, the teachings. Then they share this with us. So we believe they have a great pearl, a great treasure to share with us."

"So all Buddhists have to do is give some food and you're OK, is that it?" asked Andy.

"No. There is much more than that," replied a rather cross David. "We try to live simply too and not to take life."

"I don't really understand all this fours and eights," said Joanne. "Can I borrow the book you mentioned, Anna?"

So the five of them went back to David and Anna's house. When Anna and David's mum came in from work, they were sitting in the kitchen looking through a whole pile of books.

"Well, well, well," said Mrs. Ford. "Looks like a library in here."

They all explained what had happened and why they were looking through the books. Then Steve really got the conversation going.

"Seems to me Mrs. Ford, that practising Buddhism is all very well for the monks, but what does it offer to someone like you? You're a successful woman, why do you need Buddhism?"

Mrs. Ford sat down at the table to chat.

"I expect Anna has told you about the Eightfold Path. Now, there are some very practical rules for someone like me with a small business. One of the parts of the Eightfold Path is about 'right livelihood'. That means that whatever job you have, it must be a good one. It must not involve harming humans, animals or nature. The work should help nature. You must not have anything to do with selling weapons, slaughtering animals for meat, selling poison, alcoholic drinks or drugs and in no way must you deal with anything which makes slaves of people".

"Slaves!" said Joanne. "Not many slaves round here, Mrs. Ford!"

"Not in the old fashioned sense of the word, but there are many people who are slaves to their jobs, or their families," commented Mrs. Ford. "Has Anna or David told you about the Five Precepts?"

"The Five Prefects?" asked a very confused Andy.

"No, no," replied Mrs. Ford, "the Five Precepts. These are the five sort of promises that we take as lay Buddhists. Monks hope to become like the Buddha and to achieve 'Enlightenment' by fully understanding what we are and why we are here. But ordinary Buddhists like me can't hope to do that. So we follow the Five Precepts.

"We try to live our lives in such a way that we obey these rules and bring peace and compassion to others. The Buddha gave some guidance for ordinary people. He taught that everyone should try to work hard and provide themselves with enough to live comfortably, but not extravagantly. He taught us that we should care for those who are poor. The Buddha saw that poverty leads to theft and crime. This leads to violence and lies and so suffering is increased for everyone. So a society should try to get rid of poverty and make sure everyone has enough to live on."

"But what I might think is enough to live on might be more than you think!" said Joanne. "So who decides?"

"Good question, Jo," said Mrs. Ford. "Buddhists believe you cannot make laws to control this. You have to show an example. So we try to live, comfortably but simply. And that brings us back to the monk in the woods. He shows us that even our way of life might be too comfortable! He makes us think about our priorities and how we should spend our time, our money and our energies. But enough of this! Anyone for some cake and biscuits?"

# THE BUDDHA

Siddartha Gotama was the son of a wealthy Indian prince who lived near the border of Nepal two thousand five hundred years ago. He lived a life of luxury but then as a young man he suddenly saw how other people suffered. Going outside the Palace walls for the first time, he saw an old man, a sick man, a corpse and a wandering monk. As he observed the world around him he saw how everyone eventually faced sickness, old age and death. He wondered if there was a way to free ourselves from this pain and so, following the example of the monk, he abandoned the comforts of his family and home to try and find the answer to this question.

He became a wandering monk and visited the most famous religious teachers to see if they could answer his question but none of them could. He practised strict fasting and deprived himself of food, heat and comfort but this way of life was not the answer. Eventually he developed a way of life called the Middle Way, a way of life that avoids the extremes of hardship and the extremes of luxury. He ate enough to live in a healthy way and discovered how to calm his mind through a form of meditation based on breathing.

At the age of thirty-five, on a full moon night in May, Siddartha found what he was looking for. As he sat under the sacred bodhi tree, calming his mind with meditation, he saw the truth and experienced absolute release from the pain of sickness, old age and death. At that moment he became the Buddha, the Enlightened One. He would no longer be subject to the cycles of birth and death that tie us to this world. For the remainder of his life he travelled India on foot, teaching and helping others to attain Enlightenment and when he died he left his teachings, the Dharma, as a guide for those who follow him, and his group of followers – monks – as a permanent community who would keep his teachings alive.

♦ *Thai Buddhist Forest monk working on a reforestation project.*

♦ *The Buddha.*

# THE FOUR NOBLE TRUTHS

The Buddha realised that our life is one of suffering and that we ourselves create this suffering. We are afraid to let go of our feelings – when we are angry we think it will last forever, just as when we are happy we never want to be sad again. The Buddha said that everything comes and goes, that we shouldn't try to hold onto the things that we like or turn away from the things that cause us pain. The Buddha said that once we understand the Four Noble Truths we can truly begin to follow the Path that he taught.

The First Noble Truth – Suffering exists.

The Second Noble Truth – There is a reason why we suffer.

The Third Noble Truth – We can escape this suffering.

The Fourth Noble Truth – The way to escape this suffering is by following the Noble Eightfold Path.

# THE NOBLE EIGHTFOLD PATH

The Buddha taught the Eightfold Path as a way of life for all people. The eight branches of this Path are:

1. Right Views – to have an open mind, to think of the good things in ourselves and in other people.
2. Right Thoughts – caring for others, being sympathetic and nonviolent.
3. Right Speech – not telling lies, not gossiping, thinking before you say something hurtful or stupid.
4. Right Action – do not kill or cause injury, do not steal.
5. Right Livelihood – do not have a job which cheats others, avoid jobs which involve using or working with weapons or armaments, making or selling drugs or alcohol, killing animals or causing suffering to others.
6. Right Effort – work hard to avoid straying from the Eightfold Path.
7. Right Mindfulness – be aware of your own thoughts and actions – these affect the world around us now and in the future.
8. Right Concentration – this is the peaceful state of mind that should arise if we have followed the Noble Eightfold Path.

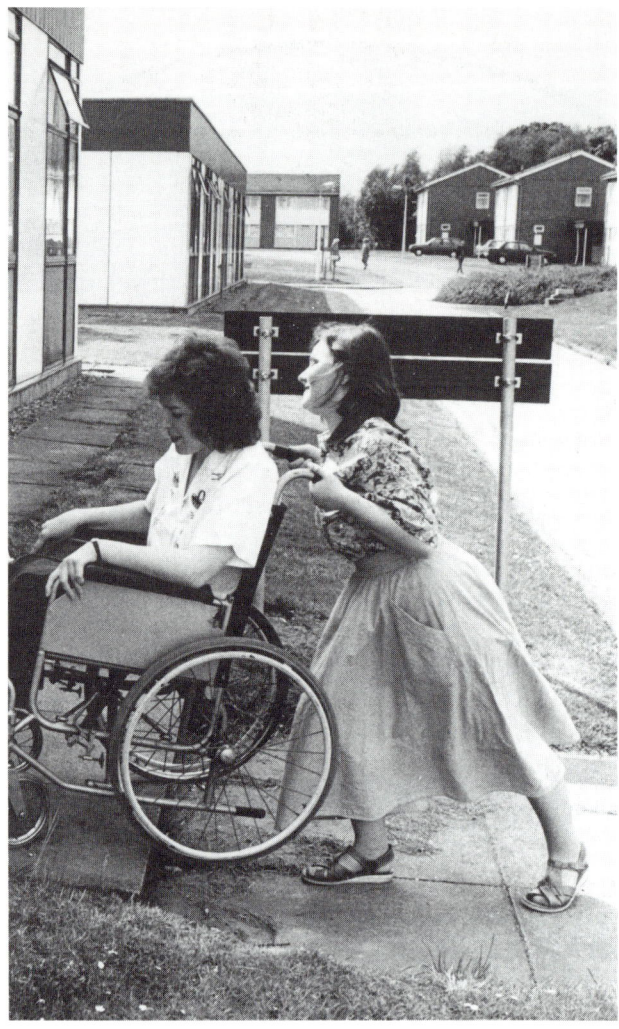

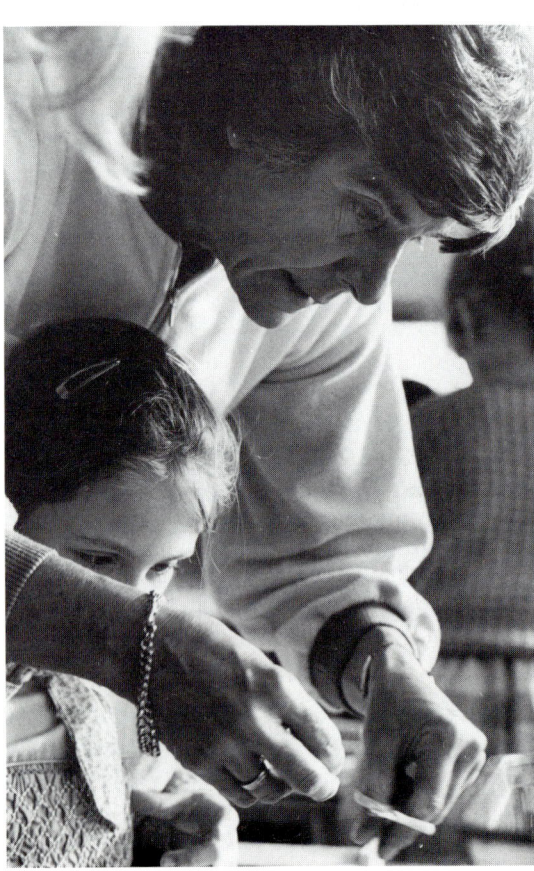

# THE FIVE PRECEPTS

Among the many teachings that the Buddha gave he asked those who followed his path to try and live according to the advice contained in Five Precepts.

These are the Five Precepts:

1. A follower of the Buddha should be sympathetic and helpful to all things that have life and should always be careful not to harm or kill humans or living creatures.
2. A follower of the Buddha should not steal or take what has not been given freely by others and should at all times be generous to those who are poor or in need.
3. A follower of the Buddha should be restrained and not take more than is needed whatever he or she is doing.
4. A follower of the Buddha should avoid telling lies and speaking ill of others.
5. A follower of the Buddha should try to speak the truth, use only kind and gentle words, speak in a way that encourages peace and choose words that suit the people and the place where he or she is speaking.

The Buddha's teachings are a guide to life and a Buddhist will try to follow them at work and at home, with other people or alone.

## KARMA

Buddhists believe that we are tied to a continuous circle of rebirth and at death we can be born into another life. The Buddha said that because we hold onto greed, anger, desire, hatred and other emotions we cannot really see the true nature of things. We become so tied up in our emotions that we harm ourselves or others by our words and actions. When we do this we create a force that ties us to the continuous circle of births and deaths. This force is called karma. Our everyday actions create karma and this karma is carried through into our next life. But if, during our lives, we understand the Four Noble Truths and find a way to free ourselves from the suffering of life, we can break free from the continuous circle. When we let go of desires and emotions and truly understand the Buddha's teachings we do not create any karma so the force becomes less strong and eventually it no longer exists. When this happens we are eventually free of this world and of all other worlds. This freedom from all ties is called nirvana and it is the stage when all our needs and wants are cooled or put out like a dying flame. It is the aim of every Buddhist to achieve nirvana in this or in another life and it is the reason why the Buddha gave his teachings.

◆ *Buddhists believe that until we can let go of the sense of self that keeps us tied to this world we pass through many cycles of birth, growth, decline, death and rebirth.*

## BUDDHISM AT WORK

Buddhists believe that we have been born many times before and we will have to pass through many other lives until we truly understand the Four Noble Truths and follow the Eightfold Path. Ordinary people can attain enlightenment, just as the Buddha did, but until we are ready for this we have to apply the Buddha's teachings in our day-to-day life. It is possible to calm the mind through hard work and it is wrong to create jobs that are boring or harmful for they disturb our peace of mind and make us angry or dissatisfied.

Buddhists are advised to avoid work that involves killing or torturing animals, harming humans or making weapons. The most fruitful work is work that is shared with others. Buddhists support co-operative work. In this type of work the decisions, the responsibilities and the profits are shared by all the workers. The Buddha's teachings require us to think before we act, to realise the effect that our work has on others, to stop work if it is harmful to others and to give alms to those in need.

# ACTIVITIES

◆ Buddhist monk with food offerings from lay people.

## CRAVING

Buddhists believe that we create our own suffering through our individual craving. We concentrate so hard on getting what we want that we become selfish. Our selfishness leads us in turn to hurt others and when we hurt others we create even more suffering for ourselves. The more we crave, the more we tie ourselves in a web of selfishness and confusion.

Buddhists try to free themselves from craving and suffering through love and compassion for ourselves and for others. The Buddha said that before we can help others we have to help ourselves and we have to understand the reasons why we want things and why we need them. But it is not just possessions that we want, we also want to have friends or happiness and are willing to hurt others so that we don't lose this happiness. The extremes of poverty and riches are harmful to us since the craving to escape one or to achieve the other can lead to theft, dishonesty or corruption.

Buddhists try to let the spirit of generosity rule their lives and not the spirit of selfishness. The Buddha said that we are here to give to others but we should always remember that everything here is not real, it is only temporary.

## MONKS AND ALMS

At his death, the Buddha gave his teachings to the community of monks and nuns known as the Sangha. They are people who have chosen to live as closely as possible to the Buddha's teachings. Not everyone wants to live the way that they do and not everyone is ready to live this way. Monks and nuns rely on members of the lay community for their food and clothing. The Buddha was once asked by a king what a monk needs to be contented. The Buddha replied that the monk only has four basic needs for survival:

1. Food which they must be given freely.

2. A set of three robes.

3. Shelter for one night.

4. Medicine for illness.

Many monks and nuns live in monasteries which are paid for by the local community.

People come to the monastery to meditate, listen to the teachings or ask advice. They give whatever money they can afford, to the monks. Buddhist monks and nuns try to avoid handling money since whatever they need is given to them by other Buddhists. Not all monks, however, live in monasteries. Some monks live in villages and others travel, teaching where they stop and accepting what they are offered by the local people. In Thailand, all teenage boys are expected to stay at a Buddhist monastery for at least three months to work on the monastery land and to study with the monks.

After the three months have passed the boys are free to return home or to continue their studies in the monastery.

In Thailand, the Forest monks spend three months a year — in the rainy season — in private prayer and meditation alone in the forests.

**A C T I V I T I E S**

**1.** Buddhism teaches that everything we do, has its own result, or consequence. Copy this chart and fill it in for the past two days:

What have been the effects of these actions

|  | on you | on other people | in the short term | in the long term |
|---|---|---|---|---|
| Someone I was nice to |  |  |  |  |
| Someone I was angry with |  |  |  |  |
| A decision I made |  |  |  |  |
| What I spent money on |  |  |  |  |

**2.** Buddhism teaches people to gradually free themselves from their desires – from wanting things.

Chose two things from each of these lists that you would be willing to give up:

- television
- a hobby or a sport
- pocket money
- radio or stereo
- your favourite food

- friends
- being in a team or a club
- free time at the weekend
- spending time with your family
- talking and laughing

How will this affect you?
How will this affect others?
What will you replace it with?

If these things were taken from you what would you pay or do to get them back?

**3.** Why do Buddhists think it a privilege to give to monks and nuns?

Is there something that you or your family or your school give money or time to, where you are not buying something, but you feel it is time or money well spent? Write and illustrate what this is and try to explain the reasons for giving your time and/or money.

**4.** Read the section on 'Buddhism at work'. What job might you do when you leave school? Does this job fit in with Buddhist teaching? If not, could the working conditions be changed to make it fit in better with Buddhist teaching?

◆ *Shrine to Mary Mother of the Sea and Jesus at a quayside in Northern Greece.*

# CHRISTIAN STORY

Jackie's mum had said there would be a special guest for lunch. It was to be the preacher at church. While her mum had gone to church Jackie had stayed in bed and when she went down for breakfast there was a message from her mum asking her to tidy up the house before the visitor arrived. Once she had finished cleaning she settled down to read a magazine.

She must have fallen asleep because the next thing she knew her mum was shaking her gently to wake her up.

"Jackie, I'd like you to meet Rev. John Mwese."

Jackie's jaw dropped and she just remembered to murmur,

"Pleased to meet you."

A tall African man stood in front of her, dressed in white clothes and wearing a white cap. This was not the sort of preacher Jackie had expected! The visitor smiled broadly.

"Actually, my full title is High Priest John Mwese – but please call me John," he said.

Soon the room filled with other people from the church who Jackie's mum had invited home to meet John. The noise of people talking excitedly soon filled the room. It was obvious that John's sermon had interested many people.

Before lunch, the issues came out. John is the head of a church in Africa which is called an 'indigenous church'. This means it was not founded by a missionary from the West but by Africans themselves.

"So you see, we have never felt 'owned' by the West. We never had any money from outside our own area. Everything we built, we built through our own efforts. We are proud of that."

"What are you doing here in England?" asked Jackie.

"Well, I'm here as a guest to see how your churches work. I want to see what I can learn and maybe there are some things I can share with you."

"Like what?" asked Jackie, ignoring her mother's angry looks. Other people were waiting to speak to John but Jackie was interested now.

"I gather from your mum that quite a lot of young people around here are unemployed," said John. "In my town it's the same. Good men and women with no jobs. So in our church we make sure that such people are the ones we ask to help us build or repair, help run clubs or look after the elderly. We don't have much money. But we all have skills and something to give."

One of the other guests, a local businessman, butted in as John was speaking. "Obviously you don't let people be scroungers, living off other people. Good thing, too. The Church should tell people to get up and find work in my opinion."

Jackie could see that this angered John, but when he spoke it was very quietly.

"No, no. You misunderstand me I think. We are all scroungers. We usually live by living off other people. You told me you sell caravans. Well, are caravans really necessary for most of the people you sell them to? Probably not. Surely as Christians we know that we really own nothing. Everything comes from God and every-thing will return to God. In our church we try, not always very successfully, to work together, using whatever God has given us and putting that together."

Jackie's mum broke in here. "Give us an example of what you mean, High Priest."

"My local church," said John, "is building a refugee centre because so many people have fled from one of our neighbouring countries due to war and famine.

We decided to build a centre for these people. Now there are three regular ways that people give gifts of money or goods to the church. There is the tithe – we give a percentage of what we earn or farm. So I get paid money by the church. I give 10 per cent of that a year to my local church. But perhaps one of my neighbours, Mrs. Wanjia, has no real money, but she grows crops on her plot of land. She gives 10 per cent of her beans. Because there are more than a dozen people who give tithes of beans, the church is able to sell a large stock of beans regularly on the market and can earn money that way.

"Secondly, we give money or gifts as a thanksgiving. God gives us so much. How good it is to give when times are good. Thirdly, if there is a special need in the community, we also give money or gifts then."

"It's a bit like a better organised collection plate?" said Mrs. Armstrong, the treasurer of the church.

"No, it's more than that. You see, when we came to build the centre, we had enough money for most of the raw materials but not all – so

people who make nails gave us some nails. The town carpenter gave wood. And our young unemployed gave their energy and strength. In return we gave them some money, food and a sense of belonging. I wonder, Mrs. Armstrong, what does your church ask Jackie to give and what does her church offer back to her?"

Jackie felt she had to answer, "Sounds nice, but isn't it really just cheap labour?"

"It can be, but we hope not. Where I live money is not everything. Respect, a sense of belonging, food, shelter, friends – all these are just as important. In our church we are nearly all poor. But that is only if you look at what money we earn. We are rich in skills, strength, patience, energy and friendship."

"Does that mean you built everything yourselves?" asked Mr Graham, one of the churchwardens.

"Nearly everything. We couldn't build the medical equipment for the clinic at the centre. So through our national Council of Churches, we asked Christian Aid in England for funds to buy equipment. The equipment is mostly made in Africa, but is far too expensive for us to buy."

"That's easy for you to do," said the businessman, "but surely Christ said you will always have the poor with you. Don't you think the Church should stay out of economics and politics and just preach the word of God?"

"But what is God's word?" said John. "When Christ began his ministry he quoted from Isaiah, 61: 1-2: 'He has sent me to bring the good news to the poor, to proclaim liberty to captives and to the blind new sight, to set the downtrodden free.' Christ believed that this was his message and who am I to disagree?"

"Actually, we have some examples a bit like yours," said Jackie. "Tell Rev. John about the Inner City Fund, Mum."

So her mum told John how the Church of England was linking wealthy suburban and rural parishes with inner city parishes so that the wealth and skills of the whole Church could be shared and help the poorer ones.

"For instance," she said, "in Bristol there is a thing called Communities Organised for a Greater Bristol – COGB for short. This brings together twenty-seven organisations – most of them Christian – to try and bring combined pressure on business and the Council to improve people's lives. They have got a factory to spend £2000 making its machinery quiet so families nearby are not kept awake at night. It has brought people and planners together to improve road safety and it has persuaded the big local building society to give one percent of its profits to provide shelter for the homeless."

"The parishes with lots of money help the poorer ones. In the process, different communities learn more about each other."

"Then there's Christian Aid and Traidcraft," said Mrs. Armstrong. "You mentioned you had received help from Christian Aid. Well in this diocese we give money but we also give our time to do door to door collecting and other fundraising. At the same time we also receive. The diocese has a grant to help fund a centre for unemployed people housed in an old church. They produce all sorts of useful things for old people, like special chairs or tables."

"I never knew that," said John. "So we really are very similar. Why, I expect the lunch we are going to have will be shared together in the same way that we share our food when we have guests." But Mrs. Porter had only cooked for John and her family, she hadn't expected so many people. Then John looked around and saw the embarrassed look on the faces of the other visitors.

"Well, maybe it's an idea you could think about," he said.

# GOD THE CREATOR

Christians believe in one God who created the universe and all life. They believe that God has become known to us through Jesus Christ, the Son, who came to earth as a man and died for the sake of all humanity, and through the Holy Spirit who helps and guides people and is always with each one of us.

God created the earth and it is God's and although human beings were created to use and enjoy God's creation, they do not own it. Christians use the idea of a steward (someone who looks after a property for someone else) to describe how we should handle our wealth and all that God has given us to care for. Christians believe that we have been put in charge of the earth, but only in order to take care of it for the good of all. Everything we have, our food, clothes, houses, money, really belongs to God. God has trusted us with these things to make the best use of them.

◆ *Working donkeys are cared for by the Catholic Church in Lamu, Kenya.*

# THE CHURCH ON EARTH

Christians believe that they, the Church (which means all Christians everywhere and throughout all time), have to carry on the work which Jesus started when he lived on earth. The Church is sometimes called 'the body of Christ', and Jesus is thought of as the head. The head decides what should be done, but the rest of the body, the arms, legs, hands, etc., must do the work. This is why many Christians are involved in work to help the poor and the sick, because this is what Jesus did when he lived on earth.

Just as the different parts of the body have different functions, so there are many different ways of being part of 'the body of Christ', and Christians sometimes disagree with each other about what they should do. Some give one-tenth of their income to charity. Others do not like to make a strict rule, but give generously to causes they feel are good. Others give away everything they have and live in communities who share everything, as the first Christians did. Some believe that as well as using their personal wealth in the right way, they should campaign about the way that national wealth is used.

◆ *Ethiopian Orthodox icon of the Last Supper.*

# JESUS CHRIST

God was born on earth as Jesus to show God's love to humanity. Jesus lived as an ordinary man and spent his adult life teaching and healing throughout Galilee, Samaria and Judaea. Many were drawn by his wisdom and love and crowds gathered to see and listen to him as news spread of his teachings and of the healing miracles he had performed. At the age of thirty-three Jesus was accused of causing disturbances and making false claims to be king of the Jews. He was condemned to death before an angry crowd and crucified. Jesus was buried in a tomb and a heavy stone sealed the entrance. On the third day after his death his disciples found the stone had been rolled back and Jesus had gone. Christians believe that God raised Jesus from the dead to show us that love overcomes even death and that there is life after death. Christians call Jesus 'Christ' which means God's chosen one.

When Jesus left the earth after he had risen from the dead, he left behind his disciples, those who had been with him for his three years of teaching. He promised them that they would not be abandoned but that the Holy Spirit would come to guide them. Jesus's words were fulfilled at Pentecost when the Power of God, the Holy Spirit came to the disciples as they hid in a room, fearful of the authorities. When the Holy Spirit came many extraordinary things happened. The disciples were all filled with a new courage and enthusiasm to go out into the streets and spread the message of Jesus. Not only this, the people hearing them each heard the message in their own language, because of the power of the Holy Spirit. Ever since then Christians have looked for the guidance of the Holy Spirit to know how they should follow God's will.

## THE CHURCH

The Church is not simply a building. Christians use the word to mean 'all Christian people'. The first Christians did not have a special building, but met in each other's homes and shared everything they had. Gradually the Christian faith spread, and there were Christians in many parts of the world who did not often meet each other. This was when disagreements began to happen, and over the centuries the Church has split into different groups called denominations. The different denominations agree over the essential teachings of the Christian faith, but disagree over many other points such as the ordination of women as priests or whether divorce or contraception are acceptable in the eyes of God. Even though they disagree about such matters, they all try to show God's love to the world, to the poor, the sick, the homeless and others in trouble — just as Jesus did.

## CHURCH PROPERTY

Ever since the early church, some Christians have given up their wealth to the church. For some denominations, which have been established a long time, this has meant that they have built up large stocks of money, land, and possessions. These are often used to help pay for the work of the church and to pay the salaries of its leaders. But some Christians believe that the church should not own such large amounts of wealth, or should use them differently. Throughout history there have been individuals and religious communities who have tried to follow God's teachings and example by living a life of strict poverty and humility. By giving away what they own and dedicating their life to the care of those who need help they believe they can be truly close to God.

## ACTIVITIES

1. Choose one church from your local area and find out:

   a) What does the church offer to the community? (For example, a place to meet, counselling for those with problems, looking after children and young people.)

   b) For which of these services (not the worship services!) does the church charge money? (for example church hall rents.)

   c) Which of these services are available from other organisations?

   d) What do members contribute to the work of the church in terms of a) money and b) time?

   e) Make a list of all the resources (for example, buildings, money, staff) that the church has. How do you think these could best be used to help others?

2. High Priest John in the story tells how Jesus began his work by reading from Isaiah. Read Luke 4, 16-21.

   For each group mentioned in the passage from Isaiah, find a group of people in the modern world who are in the same situation.

   Then read Matthew 25, 31-46, and again, find an example of those who are hungry, or thirsty, etc. Some of these may be the same as your first list.

   For each group, write down what you think Christians should be doing to help.

# ACTIVITIES

**3.** Write down how much money you get every week (pocket money or from a job).

Copy the chart and fill it in for a week to record how you spend your money.

| Money | Mon. | Tues. | Wed. | Thurs. | Fri. | Sat. | Sun. |
|---|---|---|---|---|---|---|---|
| Spent on yourself. | | | | | | | |
| Write down what you bought. | | | | | | | |
| Saved for something you want | | | | | | | |
| Given to others | | | | | | | |

Of the things that you have bought this week, how many of them have you still got at the end of the week?

What are you saving?

What did you throw away?

If you gave some money away – how was it used?

Would you want to give any of your money to help the work you suggested in 1 and 2, whether through a church or other religious or non-religious organisation?

**4.** Find out from other people in the class what their hobbies or talents are.

Put this information under the correct headings below:

Hobbies that involve making something:

Hobbies that involve musical instruments:

Hobbies that involve sport:

Hobbies that involve collecting something:

Hobbies that involve helping other people:

Other hobbies or skills:

What are the things that your class could do for others that involves using these hobbies or skills? Could any of these skills help the work that you suggested in 1 and 2 whether through a church or other religious or non-religious organisation?

◆ *Tractor waiting to be blessed at a Harvest festival in Nairobi, Kenay.*

◆ *Christian open air bookstall outside a church in Nairobi, Kenya.*

# HINDU STORY

As the bus drove on Gopal could see the huge temple spires looming up over the flat countryside. They must still be about fifteen kilometres away, he thought. On either side of the road were flat fields dotted with clumps of trees, mainly palms. In the fields Gopal was surprised to see how many people were at work: women wading among the rice-paddies, or carrying loads on their heads; men walking behind pairs of oxen ploughing the fields, or driving oxcarts laden with produce through the network of fields and ditches. Every few minutes the bus would stop, and more people would climb aboard. Often they were carrying baskets of vegetables or sacks of grains.

One man had with him about ten bundles of what looked like leaves, all tied up into tightly bound packages, which he balanced on the seat next to Gopal. As the bus careered round a corner it hit a particularly bad bump and several of the bundles of leaves, or whatever they were, came tumbling all over him. One of them broke open and scattered across the gangway. It was then that he saw that they were actually hundreds and hundreds of round mats, each one made of several large leaves cleverly woven together.

"What are they, Dad?"

"They're plates. You only use them once, and then you throw them away. But because they're made of leaves, they rot straight back into the earth. And you don't have to waste water washing up . . ."

"No washing up! Mum'd like that!"

"Yes, so would I – it would save hot water. That's the Hindu way of life – keep things simple and don't waste anything."

Eventually the bus arrived at Srirangam and pulled to a halt in front of one of the towering temple gates. Gopal had to wait patiently while the bundles of leaf-plates were unloaded along with all the other assorted baggage and people on board. At last he was able to clamber out into the hot sunshine.

Gopal and his father walked towards the huge temple gate. Gopal could see layer upon layer of intricately carved arches and ornaments towering into the sky, at least sixty metres high. Before them a cool dark tunnel led past enormous wooden gates into the famous temple of Ranganath, around which the town of Srirangam was built.

At the other end of the tunnel waited Narasingha Bhatta, the headmaster of the temple school. He greeted them and showed them round the temple compound. It was just like a self-contained town, with streets and houses where all the priests and temple workers lived.

"What's this for?"

Gopal had climbed up a big square pedestal standing against one of the temple walls and was looking down into a huge round basin, measuring about four metres across and over two metres deep, made out of ancient stone.

"This is where the temple used to keep ghee," explained their guide. "Ghee is clarified butter which is used as cooking oil and to fuel the lamps. The temple used to own thousands of cows. According to Hindu tradition, cows are the sign of real wealth. They give us milk, butter, yoghurt, cheese and, most importantly, ghee. The temple used to use this much ghee every day."

"But this could hold nearly four thousand litres," estimated Gopal's dad, "That's an awful lot of ghee. In England ghee costs about £3 per pound."

"Yes. Many years ago this temple was very wealthy. Most of the ghee was used to cook for the pilgrims who came here. First the food was offered to Vishnu, and then, when it was sanctified, it was given to anyone who came. Now we still get lots of pilgrims, but we can't afford to cook in ghee any more – we use palm oil instead."

"What happened? Why did the temple lose its wealth?"

"Because people were tempted away from the traditional Hindu way of life by Western ideas," replied Narasingha. "They were told that it would be better to use their money and land to build up industry and big cities. The temples which used to be the centre of society, have now become irrelevant to a lot of people. The new temples are the universities."

"But you are the headmaster of the temple school. Won't your boys go to university?"

"Some of them will, of course, but most of them will study Sanskrit and learn how to chant the Vedic hymns. They will serve as priests in this temple and in other temples all over India. The Sanskrit writings of ancient India teach so many things – medicine, astrology, sociology, politics – and the priests have to be expert in all those subjects so that they can give proper guidance to society. But nowadays students want to go to university and learn engineering and science, so that they can make money in a professional career. As a result the traditional wisdom is being lost."

"What's that got to do with the temple becoming poor?" asked Gopal.

"Everything. The temple was the focus of rural economy. According to Hindu philosophy, natural produce of the land, such as food-grains, milk, vegetables, cotton, herbs and so on are considered as the real, God-given wealth. These should be blessed by religious ceremonies. Every home and every village has its temples, and the big temples, like Srirangam, are the place where the whole community comes for big festivals and where the produce of the whole region is offered to God. As such they should be very important in the local economy. They used to be the distribution points for the poor in times of shortages, and they became the cultural centres for the region, where education and the arts flourished. Now, with the growth of industrial cities, the temples are no longer important, and they have become poor. Industry and science are now flourishing, but the cities, where all the wealth is supposed to have gone, are poor too."

Gopal remembered Madras. A huge bustling city, two hundred and forty kilometres north of Srirangam. They had flown there straight from London. He hadn't liked it because of the noise, the crowds, the dirt and the poverty. During the four days they were in Madras he had begun to regret coming to India and wanted to go back home to London. London was a big city too, one of the biggest in the world, but London was different. It was much cleaner, there was no poverty, and it was fun.

"What's wrong with cities? I live in London and I like it."

"Ah, London. the capital of the empire! When I was a schoolboy we were taught to worship London. We used to dream of going there one day. They told us at school that Madras would become like London, and that India would one day be richer than England. We believed them then, and we all wanted to help build the new India. But it's not so simple. India's wealth is in what grows on the land. But now big businesses control the land, and the money from it does not go to the villagers, or even to Indian cities like Madras, but to London and other rich cities. They grow richer, while our villages are being destroyed."

Gopal had to think about this. It was very complicated and he wasn't sure he understood exactly what Narasingha was saying. For the rest of the walk round the temple he was unusually

quiet. When it was time for lunch their guide took them to his home. It was very simple, clean and peaceful. they sat on the floor and waited to be served. Gopal was still deep in thought.

"Dad, I've been thinking about what Narasingha said. What it means is that the reason we are rich is because these people, I mean the villagers of India, are poor. We've made them poor!"

"Yes, in a way that's true, Gopal. In an indirect way we've taken their money and used it to build big cities like London. But we haven't made them poor. They still have a great civilisation. People like Narasingha still know how to live a simple life and be happy without wasting what God gives them. There's more ways of being rich than just by having lots of money."

Gopal agreed with that. After the meal he was the first to take his leaf plate out to the yard and put it on the pile in the corner, where the dog licked it clean before it began to rot back into the earth.

# THE CYCLES OF BIRTH AND DEATH

Hindus believe in one Supreme Being from whom everything comes. All of us were originally part of that Supreme Being, but we have forgotten our real nature and fallen into the world of birth and death. Although, by nature, we are eternal spirit, called atma, without beginning or end, we are forced to be born again and again in this world and to experience life without God because of our careless or destructive actions. In our next life we will have to suffer the same difficulties that we have caused to others, and we may even be born into a lower species of animals or plant. But if we do good, we will be rewarded in our next birth with a happy life and may be born in a higher realm as a heavenly being or deva. However, as long as we remain in the illusion that we are the owners of this world and want to enjoy it, whether we are good or bad, we will have to carry on being born in this world of birth and death to live out our desires.

Hindus use the example of a tree to explain this world. The root of the tree is God, and the branches and leaves of the tree are the people and things of this world. It is no use watering the leaves and branches of a tree – we must water the root. Similarly, if we want to benefit ourselves and others, we must serve the root of all existence – God. Hindus call God by many names, such as Krishna, Vishnu, Rama or Shiva, and

♦ *Woman performing puja in the grounds of a Hindu temple, acknowledging the spirit of God in all living things.*

they believe God has many faces, but is ultimately One. They believe that all the religions of the world are worshipping the same God, but that they are following different paths to the same goal of love for the One God of all people.

Human life gives us the chance to be free from the cycle of birth and death. Eventually we will come to learn that everything belongs to God, and therefore we will no longer wish to control this world, but rather want to use it to serve the Supreme. Then we will be freed from the cycle of birth and death and can gain the state of moksha, liberation from all suffering, as eternal spiritual beings united in love with the Supreme Being, the original source of our existence.

♦ *Shiva, Lord of the Dance.*

# THE FOUR VARNAS

Traditional Hindu society was divided into four varnas or social divisions:

   the priest/teacher (brahmin);
   the soldier/ruler (kshatriya);
   the teacher/farmer (vaishya);
   and the labourer/craftsman (sudra).

These are compared to the head, arms, stomach and legs of the body. Each of them has an important role to play but cannot do it without the help of the others.

The duty of the Brahmins is to teach and give spiritual guidance – they are compared to the head; the duty of the Kshatriyas is to protect and govern – they are compared to the legs; the duty of the Vaishyas is to provide food and wealth for society by trading and farming – they are compared to the stomach; and the duty of the Sudras is to work to assist the other three varnas, working on the land, in arts or crafts, or in manufacturing the necessities of life. Each person has their own duty to do, and by doing it to the best of their ability they are serving the needs of the whole social body. There should be no-one who is considered superior or inferior – all are necessary for each other's survival.

Traditionally, although the Brahmins are the teachers and therefore the leaders of society, they are not the richest, because a brahmin must only be supported by charity – they cannot receive a wage. Therefore brahmins are often poor. But although they are poor they are highly respected. For the Hindu, a simple life is the best life, because it takes the least from the world.

Hindu culture has always glorified those who lived simply. Krishna lived as a cowherd, and the great sages live in the forest or mountain caves. Peace comes to those who have the fewest wants or needs. They believe that a simple life is the best, and extra comforts inevitably bring with them the price of added complications. For this reason Hindus have seen little reason to change their traditional life patterns except through outside pressures from the West.

The varna system is many thousands of years old. In the course of the last thousand years, because of repeated invasions, first by Muslims and then by the British, the system began to collapse. In the course of time it became corrupted by selfishness into what is today called the 'caste system', where a person is forced to belong to a particular caste just because they were born into it. Others, who are born outside the castes are branded as 'outcastes'. Instead of being a way to help everyone work in harmony the caste system has been used to keep people in their place and achieve power over them.

◆ *Hindu priest helping in a tree nursery.*

◆ *In the caste system, every family has a particular occupation.*

# INFORMATION

## SIMPLE LIVING, HIGH THINKING

Hindus believe in simple living and high thinking, not high living and simple thinking! Earning money and getting rich are not bad but should never be aims in themselves. Hindus believe that real prosperity comes from pleasing God, who can give us everything we need through the bounty of nature. They would rather be content with a simple life than be greedy for more than they need.

♦ *Unexpected visitors are welcomed by Hindus, whether at the temple or at home.*

## 'ATITHI' — THE UNEXPECTED GUEST

Hindus love to feed guests. So much so that a long-standing Hindu custom is that a place must always be left at the table for the 'atithi' — the unexpected guest. No such guest, even a beggar at the door, can ever be turned away without being fed. The custom goes further — the best kind of guests are the 'atithi', because it is said that they always bring good fortune to the houses they visit.

## COW PROTECTION

Looking after cows is an important duty for all Hindus, but it is not simply a religious duty — cows and bulls are very valuable economic assets. The cow eats anything of vegetable origin (even paper if there's nothing else!) and turns it into milk, from which comes yoghurt, cheese and the most precious of all — ghee (clarified butter used as cooking oil). The ox pulls the cart and ploughs the field to produce food grains. Milk and grains are the staple diet of village India, so the cow and bull are looked after as mother and father, because without them the villages could not survive.

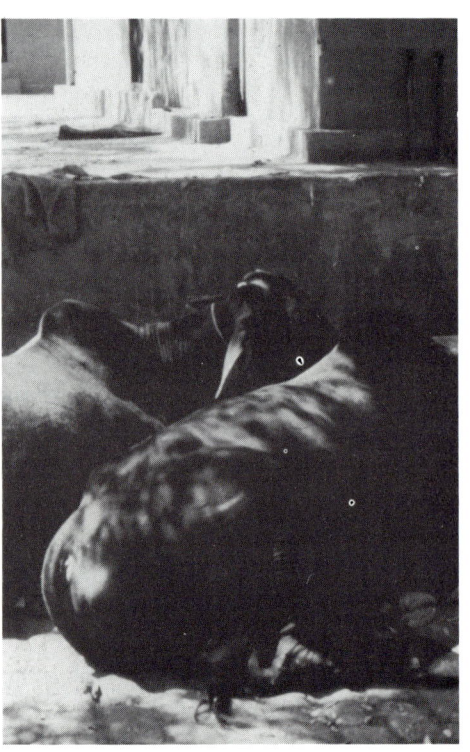

## INDIAN TRUST FUNDS

Throughout India, trust funds have been established to help those who may need money to continue their education, to buy tools or to buy farming equipment. The money is given by the wealthy to the poor but the poor are not asked to repay this money. If, however, the poor can afford to repay this money, it is returned to the trust and given to another family who need it. Those who have been helped by the trust want to help others so although money is needed to run the trust it is really consideration for other people that makes this system successful.

◆ *Man collecting sand for village building work.*

## GANDHI

The great Indian leader Gandhi warned that if India attempted to become more prosperous by following a European pattern, it would destroy the villages where the majority of the people live.

Much of Britain's wealth has come from trading with the third world, especially India. Indian cotton was sent to Britain to be woven into cloth in huge industrial mills. Then the cloth was sent back to India to be sold, perhaps in the same village where it was originally grown. It could have been spun and woven by hand in the villages, but instead money was spent in shipping it halfway across the world and back again.

It was the villagers who paid for this, and the factory owners and businessmen who organised the manufacturing and shipping were the ones who profited from it. In the end what it meant was that the villagers paid for everyone else to get rich while putting themselves out of a job. Multiply that by the two million villages in India, and the vast range of natural products produced in them, all of which have gradually been taken over by big industry, and you can see why villagers have suffered.

Gandhi was very insistent that his followers should produce their own food and clothes wherever possible. Many people today who are concerned about justice in the way goods are produced and sold quote Gandhi's words:

"There is enough in this world for every man's need, but not for every man's greed."

# ACTIVITIES

**1.** Hindus try to live as much as possible without hurting or killing animals. Make a list of things in your life that are obtained by hurting or killing animals. Against each write down what alternatives you could use.

**2.** Compare how much Indian villagers rely on cows compared with British people. What do we use that cows provide?

**3.** Read again what Gandhi said about need and greed (see previous page).
Choose from this list what you think each family in these pictures may need. If you can think of other needs add them to your list:

If someone in both of these families was given the amount of money equivalent to a week's wages what do you think they would buy?

| | |
|---|---|
| car | free time |
| television | money |
| radio | holidays |
| holiday clothes | games |
| make-up | sports equipment |
| carpets | tools |
| shoes | help in the home |
| friendship | peace and quiet |

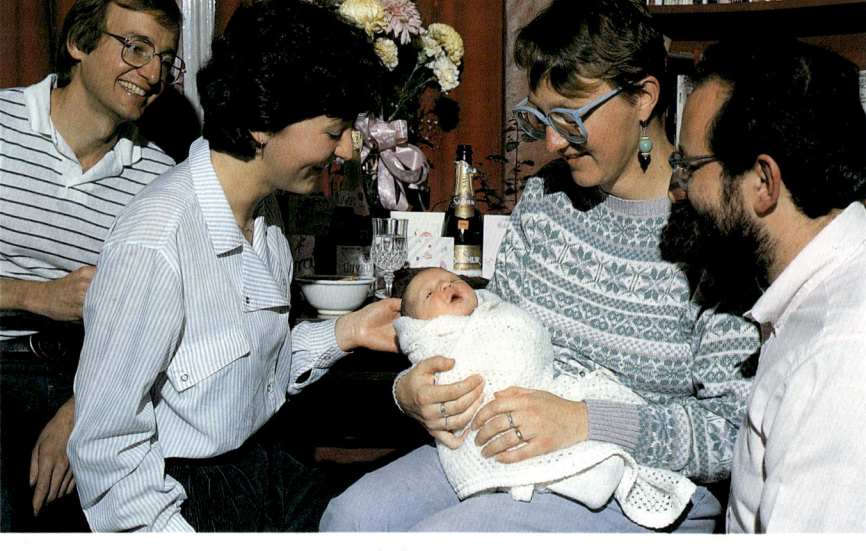

◆ *English family celebrating the birth of a child.*

◆ *Hindu family on pilgrimage in Vrindavan, India.*

**4.** The traditional Hindu division into four castes is pictured as different parts of the body. Imagine your school community as a body. Who would be the head, the stomach, the arms? What part of the body might represent the catering staff; the authority who pays for the school; the parents; the first year pupils?

What would happen if one part of the 'body' was hurt or missing?

**5.** Look at the information box on 'Atithi'. Imagine a long lost cousin turning up on your family's doorstep. He or she is without money and without a job. Write a play or a story to explain what your family would do in this situation. Make it as realistic as you can: would the family disagree about what to do? What would be the arguments?

# ISLAMIC STORY

Ayman and Omar shook hands on the deal and as they did so, they spoke together the word 'Bismillah' – 'In the name of Allah'. Theirs was an ordinary business deal, but as Muslims, they had bargained and negotiated together so that each was getting a fair deal, and Ayman was making a good profit on the sale of his vegetables. So as they completed their bargain that wet afternoon in Manchester, they recognised with the word they spoke that all wealth belongs in the end to God – Allah in Arabic. For it says in the Holy Book of Islam, the Qur'an –

'Allah owns all that is in the Heavens and on Earth'. (Surah 3:129)

Ayman left Omar's shop after a few minutes and yet another cup of Omar's very strong coffee, and went to his bank to pay the cheque into his account. As he came out he bumped into his friend Pete.

"Hallo, Ayman! Sticking to your bank, after all I said?" asked Pete.

"You can go on as much as you like, Pete, but I reckon my Muslim bank is more in touch with the real world than all your Western banks," retorted Ayman.

"Real world! Don't make me laugh! You must have thousands of pounds sitting in there as the result of your business, and it's not earning you a penny in interest. It's wasted. Money should be working hard, not sitting in a vault doing nothing."

"Oh, my money's working all right," said Ayman, "only it's not working directly for me.

You could say it's working for my family instead."

"What on earth do you mean?" asked Pete.

"Well, as a Muslim, I see myself as part of a great world-wide family under Allah. All Muslims are members of the same community, however far apart they live. The money in my bank, instead of sitting building up more money for me – and I have more than enough – is being lent to people both here in Britain and in poorer parts of the world. Every day there are people going to their local branch of this same bank and borrowing money, free of interest, to buy tools, transport, seeds, raw materials, whatever they need to set up in business. If they couldn't do this how could they survive? They would have to rely on help from others, if they can find it.

"Listen, I read about a case only the other day, about a woman called Habiba. Her husband has died and she has three children to care for. Her country has suffered a lot from famine and

What sort of tools; what kind of stone; who should carve, who polish, who keep the books. The bank then gave the villagers a loan. The villagers worked out with the bank that if they paid a quarter of the loan each year for four years, they could make enough to live off and also repay the loan. The bank didn't charge interest, so there was no problem of having to pay back more than they had borrowed."

"Well, I can see your point, Ayman. At least it's a fairly painless way of giving to charity. What you've never had you don't miss, eh?" said Pete.

"No, that's not it at all, Pete! We don't see putting our money in a bank that doesn't pay interest as charity! It is simply that the Qur'an says that Allah forbids the making of money from interest because it is money which has not been worked for and is therefore not yours to keep. All money should be worked for and made honestly. Interest, or usury, is strictly forbidden in Islam. That's why I won't use credit cards – they only operate by charging interest.

"No, charity is something else again. I give money to good causes, the same as you do. But as well as that, there's a special contribution that all Muslims give once a year at the great festival of Eid-ul-Fitr. We call it zakat, and all Muslims give a percentage of their wealth. The money goes to help the poor all over the world.

"That's what I meant when I said that my bank is more in touch with the real world than yours. Muslims today look at our world and feel very sad. They see the poor getting poorer because of the powerful banks charging interest to the poor countries. They see the rich getting richer and not caring for the poor or remembering that they are part of the same community. They see waste all around them. They see people, companies, industry and nations behaving as though we own the world. They see people taking and taking and never thinking about the generations to come.

"But we hope to show others, people who are not Muslims as well as Muslims who have forgotten Allah's Laws, that there is another way to live and do business, which helps all of Allah's creation."

"Well," sighed Pete, "I can see I'm not going to persuade you any different. There's plenty would say you're being a fool to yourself, but I must admit – and don't tell anyone I said so – I have to admire you for it!"

drought. Once the family had a small herd of goats, but they all died. Now Habiba has no way to make money to support herself and her children. Her neighbours are as poor as she is. One day, she had the idea of travelling to the nearby town and visiting the Muslim bank. She suggested that if the bank would lend her and her friends the money, they could buy good cutting tools and stone and they could make carved paperweights, dishes and bowls which they could sell through a friend of hers who traded with Britain where such things were popular.

"The bank liked her idea. Together with the other villagers and the trader friend, they sat together for many days and sorted out the details.

## THE PROPHET MUHAMMAD

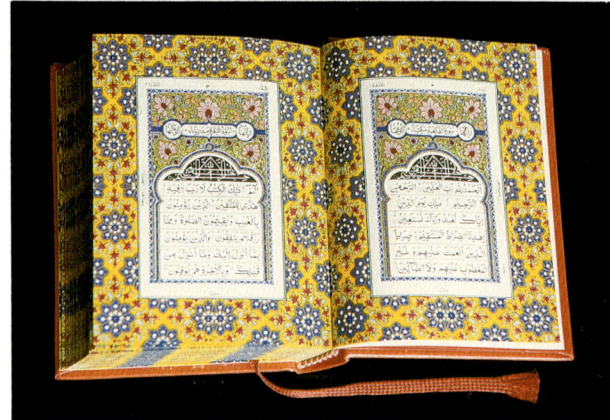

◆ *Pages of the Qur'an.*

Muslims believe that there is one God, Allah, and He has revealed His Will through the Qur'an – the Holy Book which was dictated to the prophet Muhammad. Muslims believe that before Muhammad there were many prophets – people like Abraham, Jonah, Elijah and Jesus. Each of them revealed something about Allah and His Way. But the final prophet was Muhammad.

Muhammad was born in the city of Makkah, in what is today Saudi Arabia, around the year 570 CE. When he was in his thirties or early forties he was meditating in a cave when he heard a voice telling him to recite. From that time on Allah revealed to Muhammad the words of the Qur'an, the final Book of Teachings. which Muslims believe contains all that is necessary to know how to live as Allah wants us to live.

At first most people just laughed at Muhammad, though some of his closest friends believed him. But before long, Muhammad had attracted a lot of companions and followers and the citizens of Makkah drove him out as a trouble maker. The prophet and his companions travelled north to the city of Medina. This took place in the year 622 CE. The Muslim calendar dates from this journey, known as the Hijrah. So for instance, most of 1988 was the Muslim year 1409. The Muslim year is always ten or eleven days shorter than the Western year because Muslims use the moon to record the year, while the West uses the sun.

In Medina, Muhammad set up the first mosque or place of prayer. Muslims pray five times a day and always wash carefully before prayer. After a few years, Muhammad was able to defeat the army of Makkah and re-entered the city which has become the centre of the Muslim world. It is in Makkah that the Ka'ba, the special House of Allah stands. Muslims believe that Abraham built the Ka'ba.

In 632 Muhammad died and soon his followers had spread far and wide carrying the belief in one God and in His word, the Qur'an.

## THE FIVE PILLARS OF ISLAM

There are five main things which Muslims do, which are known as the Five Pillars of Islam. These Five Pillars are like the pillars of the house which keeps it all in place. They believe first of all that there is only one God and that Muhammad was his final prophet. Secondly, they believe that they must pray five times a day. The giving of zakat which was described earlier is the Third Pillar. The Fourth Pillar is that once a year for a whole month, the month called Ramadan, Muslims fast from sunrise to sunset. This is a reminder that the material things of this world – food, drink, bodily comfort, are not the most important things. Love of God is more important and is the real source of life. Finally, all Muslims hope to go on Hajj, once in their lifetime. This is the journey made at a special

◆ *Painted wall indicating that the owner of this house in Jerusalem has gone on pilgrimage (Hajj) to Makkah.*

time of the year by millions of Muslims who travel to Makkah and go on a pilgrimage around the city and its hills.

Muslims believe that peace and fulfilment is found through surrender to Allah (Islam means to surrender or submit yourself) and that Islam offers all people a way of life which is in accord with the Will of Allah. After death there will be a Day of Judgement and those who have submitted to Allah will be granted a place in this Paradise.

## VICEREGENTS OF THE EARTH

One of the most important Islamic teachings is that Allah is the Creator of everything, and everything belongs to Him. The Qur'an also teaches that of all the creatures Allah has created, humans are the most important. The Qur'an describes Allah's decision to create human beings like this:

Behold your Lord said to the Angels: "I will create a viceregent on earth." . . . And He taught Adam the nature of all things:' (Surah 2:30 – 31).

The word viceregent is central to Islam. A viceregent is someone appointed by a ruler or king to oversee part of a kingdom. The viceregent does not own the people, for the people belong to the king and the kingdom but the viceregent takes care of the people on the king's behalf.

The Qur'an uses this idea of a viceregent to illustrate how Allah sees us and how we should care for the rest of creation. Like the viceregent, we do not own the land, creatures or things on it. We have them on trust. We may make use of them but not destroy them. We may use them but never fall into the trap of thinking we can do with them as we want. We must always remember that everything belongs to Allah. The saying, 'Bismillah' captures something of this viceregent idea. It literally means 'in the name of Allah'.

◆ *Muslim woman drawing water from the family well.*

## CHARGING INTEREST

The way Muslims do business or live should reflect this belief. As Muslims eat and drink, build and develop, farm and grow and trade and exchange, they should remember that everything is Allah's. Muslims see nothing wrong in earning money or making a profit but it should be done honestly and fairly. This is why usury, charging interest on loans, is forbidden. A bank which tries to make money for those who already have money is not putting that money to good use. No one should lose money in a bank, but neither should they make money by lending it to someone else.

This dislike of usury is one part of a wider Muslim attitude. Muslims believe that you should never have too much or too little. Usury would mean that those who have, get more. There is a story of the Prophet Muhammad washing in the middle of a river. Although he was surrounded by water he still washed out of a little bowl. His friends were a bit surprised at this and asked him what he was doing and Muhammad replied that Allah does not love those who waste the things of His Creation.

## ZAKAT

Zakat is an obligatory tax — it is the duty of every Muslim to give zakat. Zakat is payable on money earned or goods owned above a certain amount. The money that is given is distributed among schools, hospitals, community centres, families in need, charities etc. Zakat is there to make sure that what you don't really need goes to those who do need. The Muslim attitude to wealth is, not too much and not too little. The Prophet Muhammad was very careful to say that while it was good for a Muslim to become wealthy through trading skills, it was also valuable to earn money through physical labour. Islam teaches that employees must receive fair and regular wages and that an employer must care for his employees and ensure they have good clothes to wear, a decent house to live in and enough food to live on. To sum all this up, there is a saying in Islam that both poverty and wealth are a test of a person's character.

The Qur'an advises on the importance of generosity and care for those in the community. We have seen how the bank does this and how the villagers when they had enough to live on did this. In traditional Muslim villages, there was always a hostel provided for travellers to rest in free of charge. The villagers would put aside part of their crops to feed the travellers and to provide food for the wildlife. This still happens today.

♦ *Man collecting zakat outside the mosque at Eid ul Fitr.*

# ACTIVITIES

**1.** The religion of Islam forbids the charging of interest on loans. Look in newspapers and magazines and cut out advertisements for borrowing money, including 'easy payments' for goods, or investing money. Compare the interest rates in different circumstances.

How much money you would have to pay back if you borrowed £1000 for a year at 10 per cent interest? If you invested £1000 for a year at 8 per cent interest, how much would you get back?

Why does the bank charge a different rate of interest between borrowing and investing money?

**2.** How does an Islamic bank survive if it doesn't charge interest? This game will help you find out.

Study this map of the village and its surrounding area. Devise a scheme or business that you can set up in this area and which you think will make a profit. Write out your application for a loan, detailing what the money would be used for, how you would work, how many people could live from the scheme, and any other details you think would help the bank to make a decision.

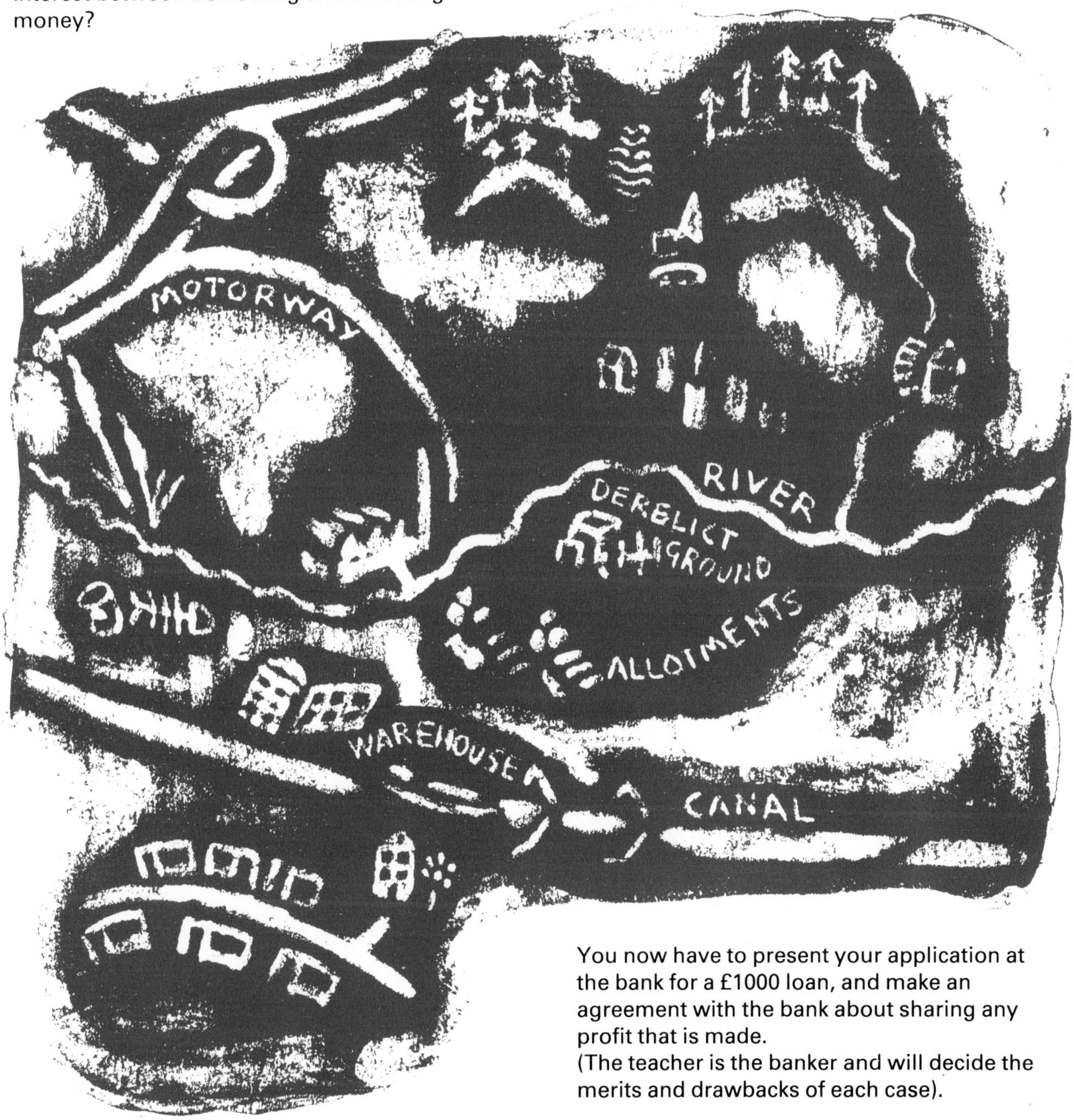

MOTORWAY

RIVER

DERELICT GROUND

ALLOTMENTS

WAREHOUSE

CANAL

You now have to present your application at the bank for a £1000 loan, and make an agreement with the bank about sharing any profit that is made.
(The teacher is the banker and will decide the merits and drawbacks of each case).

# ACTIVITIES

**3.** Muslims pay 2.5% of their wealth in zakat – a sort of 'tax' for charitable purposes. What is your wealth? How much is 2.5% of it? If your class collected this money together for charity, how much do you think you would have and what would you give it to?

**4.** Many countries in the world owe money to other countries, and have to pay interest on the loan. This is called international debt. Here are three imaginary countries. The amount that each country earns in foreign currency is also listed.

Alternia earns $5 million

Bertland earns $10 million

Redlian earns $6 million

The international debt that each country owes is written on the table below. Fill in the interest columns for repayments at 0 per cent, ten per cent, and twenty per cent. Calculate what proportion of their earnings each country has to pay back in interest at these different percentages.

◆ *Muslim women from many backgrounds celebrating Eid ul Fitr.*

**5.** What sort of banking do you think you and your family would prefer?

**6.** Why do you think Western society has developed the idea of interest so much?

**7.** Imagine you have been given £100,000 to spend. Make a list of the things you would do or buy with this money. How quickly would you spend it?
or

Imagine you have been given 100 hectares of land. What you do with this land? What would you build or plant? Who would live there?

◆ *It is believed that the Prophet Muhammad ascended to visit heaven from the Dome of the Rock of Jerusalem. This is the third most holy site in Islam.*

| Yearly interest at | 0% | 10% | 20% |
|---|---|---|---|
| Alternia owes $10 million | | | |
| Bertland owes $5 million | | | |
| Redlian owes $15 million | | | |

# JEWISH STORY

**R**euben could see the trouble coming long before it happened. For the first month of the term, it had not been too difficult. But now, with the daylight fading earlier each week, he was having to leave earlier and earlier. He could feel the others in his class becoming more annoyed. It had already been hard for him to adjust because he had been used to a different lifestyle. Reuben had been born in England but his family moved abroad when he was eleven. Now after two months in this new college his class mates were uneasy because he didn't behave like them.

One day it came to a head. The Agricultural College has a common room where all the students can go between lessons. Through the big plate glass window, you can look out over hundreds of acres of farmlands. It was a Thursday when it happened. Reuben was sitting looking out, thinking how different the scenery was from his home area in Israel. He didn't notice the three students approach him.

"Hello Reuben. Surprised to see you here. I thought you were always skipping lectures," said Tony.

"Oh don't be mean, Tony," said Alice. "I expect Reuben has some good reason for disappearing each Friday."

"Yeh, well perhaps he would like to share it with us, if he's got the time," replied Tony.

Reuben turned to face the group.

"Now you have asked, I'll be happy to explain. Won't you take a seat?"

This rather threw Tony, who sat down with a thump. Alice and Steve pulled up chairs.

"I suppose you know I'm Jewish. Well, in Judaism, we have special times when we are not supposed to work."

"Do you mean Sabbath?" asked Steve.

"Yes. Sabbath is our special day of the week when we must rest and enjoy ourselves with our families and in prayer and praise," replied Reuben.

"Well, how come you disappear on Friday afternoons then, if the Sabbath is Saturday?"

challenged Tony.

"Simple. Our day starts at sunset and ends at sunset. So Friday night is the start of our Sabbath. I have to have stopped work by the time the first stars appear on Friday night."

Even Tony looked impressed by this. But he soon rallied to the attack again.

"If everyone on the farm takes a day off how can it run efficiently?" he said.

"Oh but it does," replied Reuben. "We work a bit harder on Friday but it does mean that you have one day when you allow everything to rest – even the farm machinery! Not only that, but on our kibbutz we observe shmittah."

Reuben knew that none of them would have a clue what he was talking about.

"Oh. Yes. Really?" said Steve.

"Fancy that!" said Tony.

"What are you talking about, Reuben?" asked Alice, the only one honest enough to admit she didn't know.

"According to the Bible, the land and everything upon it belongs to God. Not to us. To God. We are simply the caretakers of it. We have to care for it for God. To help us remember this, we rest each week to show that life should not be all work. And once every seven years we celebrate shmittah. This means that in the seventh year we leave the land alone. We do not till it, or dig it or work on it in any way. Whatever grows on it naturally is a gift from God for the benefit of all. Any creature who needs it may take it, both people and animals. But we are not allowed to farm it."

"But why, Reuben?" asked Steve.

"On the seventh year we return the land to God. It reminds us that the land is God's and not ours and it allows the land to rest. It really is good farming practice because if you work land too hard, you exhaust it. By letting it rest, you help it recover from six years of growing food."

"But how does your farm survive during this shmittah?" asked Tony, genuinely confused.

"Well, my farm is rather different to yours. I belong to a religious kibbutz. That means a whole group of families all live together and share land and work together. We bring our children up together, eat together and make decisions together about our community. On the kibbutz, we follow the shmittah rule, and during the year that the land is resting, we rely on the food that we have grown and saved from previous years."

"But surely you could make more money if you used your land all the time, couldn't you?" asked Steve.

"But what is wealth?" replied Reuben. "We have a saying from one of our wise books called 'The Ethics of the Fathers'. It is carved on a piece of wood and hangs in our dining room on the kibbutz. 'Who is wealthy?' it asks. The answer is 'Whoever is satisfied with his portion'."

"That could be very selfish couldn't it?" enquired Steve.

"Yes it could. But in Judaism we are told in many stories that our work is part of a bigger

picture which is God's purpose for the world. We must work, because as one of our books says, 'Idleness leads to immorality, and Idleness leads to depression.' We all need some purpose in life, but what is our purpose? There is a story of an old man who was working hard planting a grove of fruit trees. A passerby asked him why he was doing this work, when he would never live long enough to eat the fruit from the trees. The old man replied 'Before I was born, my father and his father and his father planted trees which have fed me. Now I plant for my children, my grandchildren and my great grand children.' That is how we try to see our work and our role in life."

"This all sounds a bit heavy and dull to me," commented Alice.

"Dull! Not at all, certainly not to me. The Sabbath is the high point of the week, and we all look forward to it. One of our Sabbath songs greets the Sabbath like a Queen. When the Queen comes, no-one carries on with work – you stop whatever you were doing and celebrate. And it means that family and friends have time for each other, and time to have fun together. God knows what we need, and although we need to work a lot of the time, there need to be times when work simply doesn't enter our heads. God made a wonderful world for us to enjoy. What we must not do is destroy or damage it by what we do. There is another saying which captures that.

The rabbis – our teachers – say that on the Judgement Day, God will judge you for all the things which you could have legally enjoyed upon earth, but didn't!"

"Don't you mean the other way round?" asked Steve. "Don't you mean God will judge you for all the wrong things you have done?"

"He may well do that as well. But the saying of the rabbis means that God has created much on this earth which we are to enjoy. If we do not, if we spend all our time working or worrying or being mean or whatever, and don't enjoy this world, in a caring way, then we have failed to live as fully as God wants us to."

"That's all right for people who have money, but what about the poor?" asked Alice.

"There are no poor in our kibbutz because we share what we have. But outside the kibbutz, yes there are the poor. In Jewish society, however, you are expected to give ten percent of your income to charity. This is looked after by the synagogue. When the synagogue officials hear of a family in trouble, they can help them through the offerings of the more wealthy members. I don't think that the Jews could have survived nearly 2000 years of persecution if they hadn't had this idea of supporting each other."

A bell rang through the college, and the four of them rose and went to their next session. Later that night, Reuben heaved a sigh of relief. It hadn't been so hard as he had expected. He must remember to give special thanks to God at the Sabbath meal tomorrow night. The rain beat down outside, and Reuben smiled. Even with the weather, he thought he might come to enjoy his time in England.

# BASIC BELIEFS

# THE CHOSEN PEOPLE

◆ *The clasp of this Torah is shaped like the two stones inscribed with the Ten Commandments.*

Jews believe that God made an agreement with their ancestor Abraham, and with all his descendants. "You will be my people," said God, "and I will be your God." God promised to protect His people, and has given them laws to follow. The Jews' special task in the world is simply to live according to God's laws. The laws are contained in the Torah, the Jewish holy book. There are many detailed laws, but the most important laws are known as the Ten Commandments. God gave the laws to the Jewish leader, Moses, after God had rescued the Jews from being slaves in Egypt:

I am the Lord your God who brought you out of the land of Egypt, out of the house of slavery.

You shall have no other gods except me.

You shall not make yourself a carved image or likeness of anything in heaven or on earth beneath or in the waters under the earth; you shall not bow down to them or serve them. For I, the Lord your God, am a jealous God and I punish the father's fault in the sons, the grandsons and the greatgrandsons of those who hate me; but I show kindness to thousands of those who love me and keep my commandments.

You shall not utter the name of the Lord your God to misuse it, for the Lord will not leave unpunished the man who utters His name to misuse it.

Remember the Sabbath day and keep it holy. For six days you shall labour and do all your work, but the seventh day is a Sabbath for the Lord your God. You shall do no work that day, neither you nor your son nor your daughter nor your servants, men or women, nor your animals nor the stranger who lives with you. For in six days the Lord made the heavens and the earth and the sea and all that these hold, but on the seventh day He rested; that is why the Lord has blessed the Sabbath day and made it sacred.

Honour your father and mother so that you may have a long life in the land that the Lord your God has given to you.

You shall not kill.

You shall not commit adultery.

You shall not steal.

You shall not bear false witness against your neighbour.

You shall not covet your neighbour's house. You shall not covet your neighbour's wife, or his servant, man or woman, or his ox, or his donkey, or anything that is his.

◆ *The table is set for Passover, a festival which recalls the delivery of the Jews from slavery in Egypt.*

◆ On the Sabbath, many Jews attend the synagogue to hear the portion of the Torah for that day.

# THE SABBATH

Throughout history the Sabbath has been a day of prayer and rest for the Jewish people. After a week of work it is a time to remember God and to thank Him for everything that He has created.

Once afternoon prayers have been said on Friday in the synagogue the family try to be together to pray and share the Sabbath meal. Quite often those who are poor, who are travelling through the town or who have no family will be invited to share the Sabbath meal with a family. The Sabbath is regarded as a Queen so every effort is made to separate this day from other weekdays and to ensure that it is a happy and peaceful time. Preparations for the meal begin before sunset when the table is laid with a white tablecloth and two traditional Sabbath loaves known as challot are placed at the top of the table and

covered with a white cloth. This is a time to remember those who are less fortunate and money is put aside for charity or for the support of the synagogue.

As the day draws to a close the Friday Sabbath candles are usually lit by the mother of the house and a prayer is said over them. The candles are lit to mark this day as a special day, a day that is different from the other days of the week.

After the candles have been lit, a glass of wine is filled to the brim and a prayer of thanks, known as the Kiddush, is usually said over the wine by the father of the house.

As well as being a day of rest, time is also put aside to study Jewish holy books and many children go to the synagogue to learn Hebrew, the language of the Bible.

## BASIC BELIEFS

# THE STORY OF THE SABBATH

In the beginning God created the heavens and earth. When He said "Let there be light," there was light. God divided the light from the darkness and He named them 'day' and 'night'. Evening came – the first day had passed and God said it was good.

On the second day God said, "Let the waters be divided." God made the arch of the sky to hold back the waters from the earth and He placed some waters above the earth and some below it. But the waters didn't agree to this and they began to argue so on the second day there was disagreement in the universe.

Evening came and the second day had passed but God did not say it was good.

On the third day God said, "Let the waters under heaven come together and dry land appear." At His command the earth arose and the plants and trees grew. God saw that this was good and the third day passed.

On the fourth day God said, "Let the great light and the small light appear in heaven to govern day and night." When evening came God looked at His creation and saw that it was good.

On the fifth day God said, "Let the waters fill with creatures and the sky with birds." God saw them appear and blessed them and then the fifth day drew to a close.

On the sixth day God said, "Let the earth bring forth every kind of living creature." This happened and the earth was ready so God turned to His last task. He said, "Let us take dust and create man, Adam, to be master over all creatures." So Adam was created in the image of God. God saw that Adam needed a friend so He created a woman called Lilith from the dust. This woman was also created from the image of God but she turned away from Adam and went her own way. God then made another woman so Adam could see what He was doing but when this woman appeared Adam turned away from her. Finally, God put Adam in a deep sleep and He took one of Adam's ribs. He made a woman called Eve from this rib and He placed the couple in Paradise.

On the seventh day, the Sabbath, God finished His work and rested. Everything in Paradise was peaceful until Adam and Eve did the one thing that God and forbidden them to do. They ate the fruit of the tree of knowledge of good and evil. As a punishment God cast them out of Paradise to struggle through this life on earth.

# THE LAND

The Torah tells how God led the Jews from slavery in Egypt to the land He had promised them, the land of Israel. Many of the laws God gave them are about how to live and work in this land. Today Jews live in many different parts of the world as well as in Israel, and of course not all of them are farmers. So over the centuries wise teachers have discussed the meaning of the laws for Jews who live in different circumstances. But in everything the basic principle is that the land and all the goodness from it belongs to God, and the first produce of the land is always given to God. The Torah lays down specific rules about letting the land rest, and its ownership.

## SCHMITTAH

'When you enter the land that I am giving you, the land is to keep a Sabbath's rest for the Lord. For six years you shall sow your field, for six years you shall prune your vine and gather its produce. But in the seventh year the land is to have its rest, a Sabbath for the Lord. You must not sow your field or prune your vine, or harvest your ungathered corn or gather grapes from your untrimmed vine. It is to be a year of rest for the land. The Sabbath of the land will itself feed you and your servants, men and women, your hired labourer, your guest, and all who live with you. For your cattle too, and the animals on your land, all its produce will serve as food.' (Leviticus 25, verses 2-7)

# YEAR OF JUBILEE

'You are to count seven weeks of years – seven times seven years, that is to say a period of seven weeks of years, forty-nine years . . . You will declare this fiftieth year sacred and proclaim the liberation of all the inhabitants of the land. This is to be a jubilee for you; each of you will return to his ancestral home, each to his own clan.' (Leviticus 25, verses 8-11). The passage goes on to explain how any land sold must be returned to its original owner, so when negotiating a price the number of years to go to the jubilee should be taken into consideration, since what is being bought is the opportunity to raise a number of harvests before the jubilee.

In fact this was found to be impractical, especially as land began to be used for other things than raising a harvest, so it has never been practised.

## THE KIBBUTZ IN ISRAEL

In Israel, some Jewish people of all ages and nationalities live and work in communities that share everything with one another. A community of this sort is called a kibbutz (plural – kibbutzim) The life of the people who live on a kibbutz is guided by their wish to live equally with one another so that no-one is more powerful than anyone else and that the same food, health care and education is available to everyone. The members of a kibbutz (the kibbutzniks) elect members to take responsibility for the schools, hospital, nursery, farm, kitchens, factories etc. but no major decisions are made without agreement from other members of the kibbutz. The land, houses, factories and animals belong to everyone.

Some people spend all their lives in these communities, others come to live and work there for a few months or years. Some of the kibbutzim attract both young and old people of many faiths and beliefs who have been drawn by the shared, communal life of the communities. Other kibbutzim have a religious basis. These kibbutzim try to bring the word of God to life by working on the land and by following God's laws as written in the Jewish holy book, the Torah.

♦ *Food grown on the kibbutz.*

◆ *Girl making metal bowls.*

## LIFE ON A KIBBUTZ

The people on the kibbutz live in separate houses, in flats, or in dormitories, but everyone eats together and shares the day-to-day work. People are chosen to run the kibbutz but everybody is consulted before any important decisions are made. Everybody receives a small wage and when people are too old to work, the kibbutz provides a home, food and money for the rest of their lives.

Growing crops that are suited to the land is an important part of kibbutz life and everyone on the kibbutz takes a turn at working on the land. Children have their own small farms where they grow plants and raise animals.

As well as farming, the kibbutz runs its own school, and may have factories to produce goods that are either used on the kibbutz or sold. Money from selling goods and farm produce is used to pay for such things as electricity, telephones and school books.

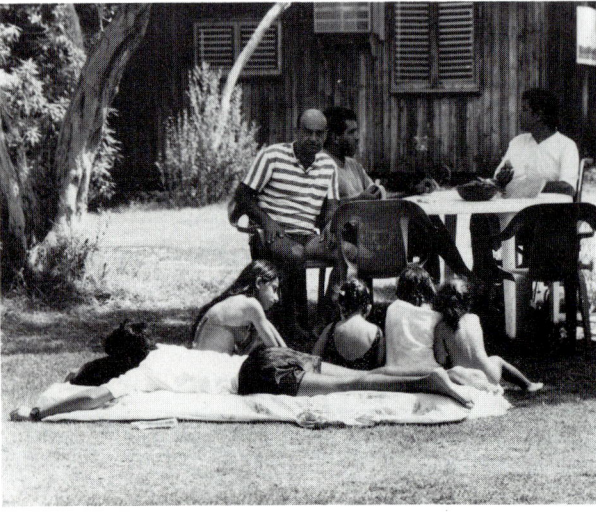

◆ *After a day's work, families have time to relax in the gardens of the kibbutz.*

# ACTIVITIES

◆ *Camels reared on a kibbutz.*

**1. a)** What happens on the Sabbath which is different from the rest of the week?

**b)** How does a kibbutz differ from an ordinary farm?

**2.** When kibbutzim were first set up they had to work out the best way of living together and working the land, and what rules to make. Imagine you are setting up a kibbutz. Look at the map of the land where you have to set up a kibbutz before you make any decisions. Working in groups, work out:

**a)** what jobs need to be done

**b)** how you would divide up the work

**c)** what wages people would be paid

**d)** what other rules would be necessary.

**3.** What do Jews believe about working for the future? Look at the story of the old man planting fruit trees.

Provide a list of things that you think you own or that have been passed down to you. List them under these headings:

Family
City
Country
World

Where do these things come from?
Are they for sale?
Which of them can never be bought or sold?
Why not?

## ACTIVITIES

**4.** Jewish law provides for a balanced division of time between work, rest, play and study. Take one weekday and one weekend day, and make a detailed record of what you did, and how much time you spent on each activity.

Then divide the activities into work (for example, helping in the house or paid work), rest, play, and study (school work). Do not count sleeping time as rest – only times when you are awake but resting (for example watching television).

Taking these two days as being typical, work out what percentage of your time is spent on each of the four types of activity. Remember there are two weekend days and five weekdays!

Make a block graph to show how your time is spent. Compare this with others in the class. Put all the results together to make a class graph.

Do you think this division of your time is about right, or would it be better if you spent more time on some things and less time on others?

## 5. PROJECT

The kibbutzim in Israel are one example of cooperative working. Find out about cooperatives in Britain or in other countries. Some are factories, some are quite small shops, some are much bigger businesses. Choose one cooperative and find out

how it was started and when

what it does

how decisions are made

how people are paid

what happens to any profit.

Is there an activity at school which runs like a cooperative?

◆ *How much time do you spend with your friends?*

52

# SIKH STORY

For once Vicky turned up on time at Rabindra's house. It was ten o'clock on Saturday morning and they had planned this shopping trip for a long time.

"Come up to my room, I'm almost ready," shouted Rabindra from the top of the stairs. "Just climb over all that stuff in the hall. As usual, Mum's up to something."

Vicky managed to squeeze by piles of brightly coloured cloth laid across the floor and was just about to run up the stairs when Mrs Singh appeared from the kitchen.

"You're just the person I need."

"Oh no," thought Vicky, "we'll never get away," but Mrs Singh guessed what she was thinking.

"Don't worry, I won't keep you long, and I'll give you a lift into town afterwards."

Ten minutes later Rabindra, Vicky and Mrs Singh were carrying out the rolls of cloth and loading them into the back of a van.

"We're almost finished. I just have to grab the orange squash and the sandwiches and we're on our way," and Mrs Singh disappeared into the

kitchen.

"What's going on?" said Vicky. "We'll never get to town at this rate."

"Wait and see. It won't take long," Rabindra reassured her.

Mrs Singh, the girls and the loaded van pulled through the gates of a local college where a small group of women were waiting. She reversed the van up to the door of a shabby single-storey building and leaned out of the window.

"Right, it's our turn now, let's get going."

As they were unloading the van, Vicky noticed men in overalls coming out of the building carrying ladders and pots of paint. Every one of the men wore a turban. Vicky finally spotted Rabindra's father amongst the men and went up to say hello.

"I see Rabindra has roped you in, Vicky.

We've just put the final coat of paint on the walls so be careful it doesn't rub off on your clothes."

"Is there some sort of party going on later?" asked Vicky.

"No, but we'll probably have one when all this is finished. The local council said we can use this building and since they don't have the money to do it up, we said we would do it ourselves. We have great plans for this building." But before Vicky could find out what they were, Rabindra landed a roll of cloth in her hands.

"All yours, Vicky. Follow me," and she headed off with her mother into the building.

A long corridor opened out into a bright room with deep windows on three sides and the sun that poured in was so bright it dazed Vicky at first.

"This is why we have the bundles of cloth,"

said Mrs Singh. "Today we are going to make curtains for each one of these windows. Sometimes the sun is so bright we can't see the blackboard and other times there's a real draught coming in through the window frames."

There were about a dozen women in the room busy rearranging the furniture and setting up sewing machines on the desks. Some of the women were dressed in a tunic and trousers like Mrs. Singh and others had dresses that reached the floor, their heads covered by a scarf.

"With all these hands it won't take us long to finish the curtains and then we can really start work," said Mrs Singh. "I hope that by the time we have finished here we will be ready to set up in business. Most of the ladies who are with us today, Vicky, are refugees from Somalia so we're running language and sewing classes."

"But I didn't know there were Sikhs in Somalia," said Vicky.

"You're right, Vicky, these ladies are not Sikhs, they are Muslim refugees from Somalia in Northern Africa, but we're here to help those who need our time and effort. It's been almost impossible for them to find work here and given that many have had to leave family and belongings behind it's hard enough already. In time we hope to set up a co-operative so we can produce our own clothes."

"But I thought you had a job already, Mrs. Singh," said Vicky.

"Yes, I do, and when the co-operative is running they won't need me, it will be their business. At the moment we are helping the women who come here to develop the skills they need to live in this country. For example, Yasmin, the lady over there with the tape measure, used to run a small business with her husband. Sadly, he was killed, but she knows how to deal with finance and has volunteered to be our book-keeper. Yasmin just needs more time to learn English."

Mr Singh appeared with a tray of glasses and a jug. "Drink up, I think you're going to need this."

"I was just telling Vicky about the project," said Mrs Singh. "You know there was a time when our parents were in the same position and in order to survive they needed the help of people living here. Now that we're settled it is our turn to help. Members of our gurdwara give their time free because it's part of our religion, in fact it's part of our way of life.

"Each morning we meditate and say the Japji prayer. This reminds us that we are only part of God's creation. We remember that in our work and in everything we do we must be honest, careful, and sharing. Here are some of the words:

'Air is Guru,
Water is Father,
Earth is Mother.
Day and night are the nurse on whose lap the whole world plays.
All good deeds and bad deeds are judged by God;
According to one's actions one is placed either near to or far from the Almighty.
Those who have meditated on God's name, worked hard and really done their duty,
Nanak says their faces are glowing,
and it is with them that many others also gain God's blessings.'

"We wouldn't be Sikhs if we didn't involve ourselves in the community. In Punjabi, we call this sewa, it means service. It's not only something we do in our free time. Sewa should be at the back of our minds when we choose a job or career.

"I know it is not always possible to give money, and really what we do is more important than giving money. Anyway, Vicky, I won't go on, I've got work to do instead. I know you want to head into town so I'll give you and Rabindra a lift. Or should I? I think you'll save more money if you stay here with us!"

# BASIC BELIEFS

## THE TEN GURUS

The first Sikh Guru or teacher was born in 1469 at a place called Talwindi in Northern India, now in Pakistan. He followed in his father's footsteps and trained to be an accountant but during this time his mind was often filled with thoughts of God. At that age of thirty, something happened to Guru Nanak – we do not know exactly what it was – but one morning as he took a bath in the river near his home he disappeared for three days. During that time the river was searched by friends and family but his body was not found. Guru Nanak appeared at his home three days later and for one day he said nothing. When he did speak this is what he said:

"There is neither Hindu nor Muslim, so whose path shall I follow?

I shall follow God's path.

God is neither Hindu nor Muslim and the path which I follow is God's."

For more than twenty years after this Guru Nanak travelled through India and other countries teaching others and encouraging them to follow God's path. The people who followed Guru Nanak's example were known as Sikhs, this is the Panjabi word for disciple. The Sikhs tried to work for the good of others as well as themselves and they followed Guru Nanak's example by beginning and ending each day

♦ Prayer at home is an important part of Sikh family life.

with prayer. When Guru Nanak died in 1539 he encouraged one of his disciples to take over his role as Guru. This disciple became known as Guru Angad. When Guru Angad died he, too, appointed a disciple to take over the role of Guru. This tradition continued and altogether there were ten human Gurus. The tenth Guru, Guru Gobind Singh, died in 1708 but he did not appoint a human successor. Before he died he said that the collection of hymns, written by six of the Gurus and Hindu and Muslim teachers, was to become the final Guru and it is now known as the Guru Granth Sahib.

♦ Pictures of the Sikh gurus are often placed near the Guru Granth Sahib in the worship room of the gurdwara.

# THE GURU GRANTH SAHIB

The Sikh holy book, the Guru Granth Sahib, is regarded as a teacher by Sikhs and is treated with the same respect and reverence as a living guru. The Guru Granth Sahib is given a room of its own in the gurdwara or in the home, in fact, any place where the holy writings are kept is known as a gurdwara – door of the guru. The Guru Granth Sahib is protected by a canopy known as a channani and wrapped in special cloths called rumala. When the book is opened it rests on three cushions on a base known as the Manji Sahib.

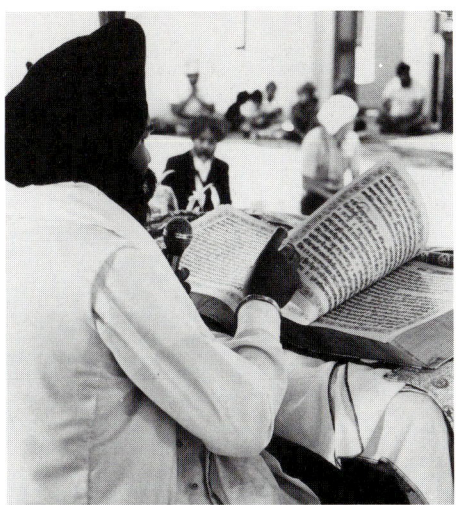

♦ The Guru Granth Sahib is read aloud in the gurdwara.

♦ There is no set age for joining the Khalsa, males and females become members when they feel ready to do so.

## THE FIVE K'S

The five signs that Sikhs wear to remind themselves and others of their faith all begin with the letter k in Punjabi, the language spoken by most Sikhs. They are:

  kesh – hair that is never cut

  kanga – a comb to keep the hair tidy

  kachera – shorts or breeches so that they will always be ready for action

  kara – a bangle of steel which reminds them that God is one, with no beginning and no end

  kirpan – a small sword or dagger which reminds them to be ready to fight against what is wrong.

## THE KHALSA

In the 17th century the Muslim rulers of India were forcing members of other religions to become Muslims and many were put to death because they refused. The ninth guru, Guru Tegh Bahadur, was one of the people who died for his faith. His son succeeded him as the tenth guru and the persecutions continued.

Twenty-four years after his father's death, Guru Gobind Singh called all the Sikhs together during the April festival of Baisakhi and asked them if they were willing to die for the Sikh faith. Five men stepped forward and the Guru took each man away. He returned five times with a bloodstained sword and the crowd thought he had killed the five volunteers. He went away a sixth time but when he came back this time all five men were alive. He called these men the 'faithful ones' and made them the first members of a group called the Khalsa, the brotherhood of Sikhs. He then decided to give himself and each of the men a name that would represent his courage. He chose the name, Singh, which means lion. He also told them to wear five signs, known as the five 'k's. Women were given the name Kaur, meaning princess.

Since that time all Sikh men and women have used these names.

♦ The turban is not one of the Five K's but is worn to keep uncut hair tidy.

## A CARING COMMUNITY

When Sikhs first came to England many of them settled in an area of west London called Southall. Most of the families had very little money and relied upon each other for help. By sharing the money they owned they were able to buy houses, renovate them and provide accomodation not only for themselves but for others who needed somewhere to live. The Sikhs also cared for the local community. They cleared wasteland, they made areas safe for children to play, they helped others build homes or set up business. Sharing and helping others was and is an important part of Sikh life and gradually Sikhs have gained a reputation as people who care for their community. As a result of their interest in the welfare of the community there are now Sikhs on the local council that decides how the neighbourhood is run.

♦ Each gurdwara has a free kitchen (langar) to which members of the community and anyone in need may come.

## EARNING AN HONEST LIVING

Sikhs believe that hard work pleases God and it is one of the best ways to put their teachings of their faith into practice. They believe that no matter how humble a job it should be done to the best of their ability.

Several Sikh stories tell of the importance that Guru Nanak attached to humble work. One day, when his close friend Lehna was carrying grass for the cattle to eat, Guru Nanak's wife reproached him for allowing such a good Sikh to do such a hard and dirty job, for the grass was muddy and was staining Lehna's clothes. Guru Nanak said, "That grass is a crown to honour the best of Sikhs."

Many Sikhs work with their hands as carpenters, builders, mechanics and, in India, as farmers. But whatever their job is they always find time to work on the building or repair of their gurdwara which is the focus of Sikh life. The gurdwara is not only a place of worship it is also a community centre where anyone, regardless of their faith, can get help. For example, if a Sikh has difficulties finding a job the gurdwara will offer work. Sometimes it is caring for the sick, organising outings for the elderly, helping those who have problems at work or offering their services in the kitchen of the gurdwara, helping to prepare the free meals that are given to anyone who comes to the centre.

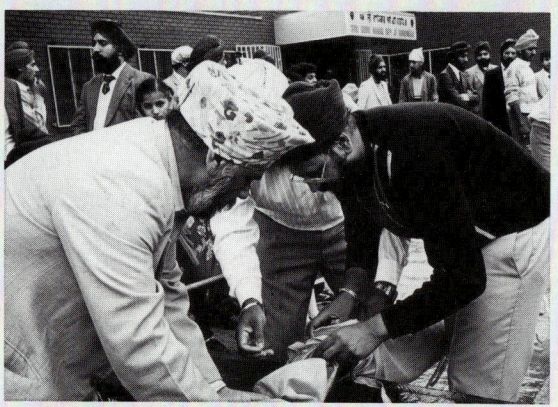

♦ Sikhs gathered outside their gurdwara to put up a new flag pole.

## ACTIVITIES

1. Make a list of the different activities that might go on in a gurdwara.

2. Sikhs believe it is important to work for others, especially doing jobs which are ordinary and sometimes not much fun. Look around you and make a list of what jobs of this sort are being done, or need doing:

   a) in your home

   b) in your school

   c) in your town or village.

   Who does these jobs?

   Do the people receive payment for their time or effort?

   If nobody did the jobs that do not receive payment, what would happen?

3. What is work?

   What do you do for friends, family and people you do not know personally?
   How many of these actions can be called work?

   What do you get in return for your efforts?

   Do you offer your work free to anyone?

Find out from others in your class if you or your parents would charge for work around the home, for friendship or company? What are these things worth to you?

4. Sikhs always share a meal after their services with anyone who cares to come. Imagine you were organising a communal meal in school for pupils and teachers.

   What food would you serve?

   Who would buy it and prepare it?

   How would you share out the work?

5. The women in this story were hoping to set up a co-operative. Try to find out more about the history of co-operatives. What are the rules that members of co-operatives follow and what type of work do they do? If you need more information you can contact the Co-operative Development Agency, 21 Panton Street, London SW1Y 4DR.

   Build up a report that looks at the work of one co-operative in your local area, one that has branches throughout the country and one that works internationally.

Where do we
go now?

I wonder what people will make of us in the future! When we look back over the past we can see how the way we live has changed, how new ideas about lifestyle and economics have affected what we do. The world has always been changing and we are now part of that process.

Old patterns of behaviour, of work, of use of money are changing very rapidly. Many of us don't often actually see money these days! We use cheques or credit cards or we ask the bank to pay money on set days to certain people like the mortgage company, the hire purchase firm, or the gas board. There is now a whole group of people who make vast sums from moving money about by telephone and fax. But is it real money? What do we mean by 'real money' these days?

At the same time, there are millions upon millions of people whose lives are made or ruined by such use of money. Ordinary people trying to make a living, while others have more money than they know what to do with. The great industrial nations meet every so often to make sure the world is running as they want it to, and the poorer nations of the world have to sit far off and try to make their voices heard. How long can we go on living like this?

In the stories you have read there are ideas, ways of living and fundamental beliefs which could offer us different choices. But they cannot do it alone. All around the world, people from all sorts of religions, cultures, ideologies and backgrounds are trying to find a new way to live – a new economics. It is possible that one system could be found to solve all our troubles. A far more likely solution is a network of different groups who work together, but each for different reasons, and who together offer the world a variety of ways of living justly.

You are part of that. Already you are an important 'consumer'. You have money and you will have more as you grow older. You will be able to choose what you do with it and how you spend it. In this book you will have found other people who have tried to stand up and do something different. The future lies with people like that, people like you.

You may feel rather helpless. But there are things you can do. Do you have a bank account or a savings account? If so, find out how your money is used by the bank or group. If you are not happy with their answer, tell them.

You are a consumer – you buy things. Look at what you buy and who produces it and where. Begin to ask questions about the way things are made and who makes money out of producing them.

Look at how your family spends its money and what resources you use. What happens to old newspapers or bottles? Are they thrown away or recycled? What foods do you buy? Who produced them and where?

Your school is an even bigger economic and social unit. Look at what the school does with its money. Does it recycle materials? How much waste is there? How does your school help the wider local community?

These are all groups you can have a direct influence upon. But there are many groups which you cannot so easily affect by yourself, or just with your friends. This is where it is important to join organisations which struggle to find more just ways of living. Development groups like Christian Aid, CAFOD, Oxfam, Muslim Aid and so forth. Environmental groups like WWF, Friends of the Earth or Greenpeace. Economic groups such as the New Economic Foundation or the Schumacher Institute. You may or may not wish to join these groups, but it is certainly worth finding out about them. Because you are going to be an increasingly important person in deciding what sort of shape our world is in over the next ten, twenty or thirty years.

*new economics*

# New Economics Foundation

New Economics Foundation is an educational charity involved in research and campaigning on sustainable economics. NEF grew out of The Other Economic Summit, which parallels the G7 summit every year, offering sustainable alternative paths for development.

Current projects and initiatives include:

◆ Formulating Alternative Economic Indicators
◆ Investigating Community Enterprise
◆ Energy Conservation
◆ Developing economic alternatives with Eastern Europe
◆ Researching links between Trade and the Environment

NEF works closely with academics and other voluntary sector organisations. Unlike ordinary economic think tanks, NEF has a membership structure which anyone can join. Members receive the quarterly *New Economics* newsletter.

For further information contact:

**New Economics Foundation**
**2nd Floor, Universal House,**
**88-94 Wentworth Street,**
**London E1 7SA.**

# Christian Aid

Christian Aid is the overseas aid and development agency of 41 churches in Britain and Ireland. It has two main tasks: first, to give support to projects in countries of the South which combat poverty and injustice and which strengthen the poor; second, to do educational work on North-South issues in Britain and Ireland with adults, students, youth groups and in schools.

For schools, Christain Aid produces regular materials for teachers. These include story and information material with related classroom ideas, videos, simulation games, posters and packs related to the National Curriculum. Two education advisers are available to run workshops for primary and secondary teachers.

For further information contact:

**Christian Aid,
Inter-Church House
35 Lower Marsh
London SE1 7RL**

**WWF**

# The World Wide Fund
# for Nature
# (WWF)

Attempts to change people's attitudes and behaviour towards the environment have often resulted in appeals being made to pragmatic or utilitarian instincts. Yet the choices we make, and the values we hold are often influenced by very different considerations – the moral and ethical, the spiritual or religious.

Recognising the importance of the religious dimension in affecting people's lives, and the power of the world's great faiths in spreading their message, WWF has for a number of years been working with different groups, encouraging them to explore their commitment to the environment and to undertake a variety of conservation and education programmes worldwide.

A Wealth of Faiths forms part of this programme of work, exploring the beliefs of six world faiths regarding wealth, prosperity, economics and values, and encouraging young people to realise their own economic importance in the modern world.

For further information contact:

> **Education Department,**
> **WWF UK,**
> **Panda House,**
> **Weyside Park,**
> **Godalming,**
> **Surrey GU7 1XR.**

# ICOREC

*international
consultancy on
religion, education
& culture*

The International Consultancy on Religion, Education and Culture (ICOREC) is an interfaith, intercultural consultancy actively engaged in promoting greater understanding and appreciation of the variety of faiths and cultures of our world. Consultants are drawn from all the major faiths of the world and represent a wide cross section within each faith. ICOREC has consultants in countries around the world as well as a home team based in the United Kingdom, and particularly at its Manchester headquarters.

The consultancy's working principle is that each faith should speak for itself in all the work which we undertake, but in a way which is accessible to others and bears in mind the audience which it is addressing. We intend that faith should speak to faith, and also that the faiths should speak to the secular world and to education.

Central to our work is the idea that religion and beliefs play a key role in shaping and giving meaning to our daily lives and the ways in which we perceive and value the world around us. To this end we deal with religion at the day to day level as well as at the philosophical and conceptual level, seeking always to acknowledge the diversity of ways in which religion and belief affect us.

Our activities range from providing photographs for publications to initiating and organising international interfaith events; from compiling essential teachings of each faith to writing interfaith philosophical studies; from producing educational materials with and for a specific faith to running cross-faith studies.

For further information contact:

**ICOREC
Didsbury Site,
Manchester Metropolitan University,
Wilmslow Road,
Manchester M20 8RR.**

# INDEX

CLEVELAND
BOTANICAL
GARDEN®